D1534712

THE END OF
OF
ASYLUM

"The U.S. asylum system has long served as a beacon of liberty for those fleeing persecution in their homelands—and for decades, enjoyed bipartisan support. As we dig out from the rubble of the Trump administration, this book is required reading to understand how his administration wrecked America's commitment to humanitarian protection. From the genesis of the asylum process to its evolution over time, Schoenholtz, Ramji-Nogales, and Schrag meticulously detail how the administration weaponized regulations, decisions, and policies to undermine this vital program. More importantly, the authors deliver comprehensive guidance for rebuilding an asylum system that again upholds American ideals and the U.S. commitment to protect refugees from terrible harm."
  —Stacey Abrams, founder of Fair Fight Action and Fair Count

The End of Asylum is an urgently needed book and a genuine public service: a meticulous account of how the Trump administration dismantled the country's humanitarian protections for asylum seekers and refugees. A clarifying read for anyone who wants to understand the full scope of the damage wrought by President Trump, this book offers a step-by-step tour of the toll for vulnerable people at the southern border and beyond. If the Trump administration's layered attacks on asylum seekers are convoluted and often legally sloppy, Schoenholtz, Ramji-Nogales, and Schrag are the opposite: clear, cogent, trustworthy guides through a bureaucratic disaster-scape. The authors remind us why refugee protections exist in the first place, tracing their origins back to moral failures during the Holocaust for which the United States, and much of Europe, sought to atone. They also train our eyes toward the future, to assess how vital humanitarian protections can be restored, or even expanded, by a new administration—a necessary spark of hope for the tempest-tossed."
  —Sarah Stillman, staff writer for the New Yorker and director, Global Migration Program, Columbia University's Graduate School of Journalism

"Concise and comprehensive, *The End of Asylum* recounts the relentless, and largely successful, efforts of the Trump administration to stop refugees and asylum seekers from receiving protection in the United States. The Biden administration should take careful note of the authors' smart and practical proposals for restoring America's traditional welcome to those seeking safety from persecution."
  —T. Alexander Aleinikoff, former UN Deputy High Commissioner for Refugees and director, Zolberg Institute on Migration and Mobility, The New School

THE END OF ASYLUM

ANDREW I. SCHOENHOLTZ

JAYA RAMJI-NOGALES

PHILIP G. SCHRAG

Georgetown University Press / Washington, DC

The publisher is not responsible for third-party websites or their content. URL links were active at time of publication.

Citations to newspapers and magazines refer to the titles and dates of their online publication, not necessarily the titles and dates in the print publications.

Library of Congress Cataloging-in-Publication Data

Names: Schoenholtz, Andrew Ian, 1951- author. | Ramji-Nogales, Jaya, author. | Schrag, Philip G., 1943- author.
Title: The end of asylum / Andrew I. Schoenholtz, Jaya Ramji-Nogales, Philip Schrag.
Description: Washington, DC : Georgetown University Press, 2021. | Includes bibliographical references and index.
Identifiers: LCCN 2020047030 (print) | LCCN 2020047031 (ebook) | ISBN 9781647121075 (hardcover) | ISBN 9781647121082 (ebook)
Subjects: LCSH: Asylum, Right of—United States. | Refugees—Law and legislation—United States. | Asylum, Right of—Government policy—United States. | Refugees—Government policy—United States.
Classification: LCC KF4836 .S374 2021 (print) | LCC KF4836 (ebook) | DDC 342.7308/3—dc23
LC record available at https://lccn.loc.gov/2020047030
LC ebook record available at https://lccn.loc.gov/2020047031

∞ This paper meets the requirements of ANSI/NISO Z39.48-1992 (Permanence of Paper).

22 21   9 8 7 6 5 4 3 2 First printing

Printed in the United States of America.
Cover design by Tim Green, Faceout Studio
Interior design by Paul Hotvedt, Blue Heron Typesetters, LLC

CONTENTS

———

INTRODUCTION

The biggest loophole drawing illegal aliens to our borders is the use of fraudulent or meritless asylum claims to gain entry into our great country.
—*Donald J. Trump, November 1, 2018, from the Roosevelt Room*

Hiring manythousands [*sic*] of judges, and going through a long and complicated legal process, is not the way to go—will always be disfunctional [*sic*]. People must simply be stopped at the Border and told they cannot come into the U.S. illegally.
—*Donald J. Trump, June 25, 2018,*
from the @realDonaldTrump Twitter account

Forty years ago, Congress passed the Refugee Act of 1980,[1] establishing for the first time a statutory process for granting asylum to people fleeing persecution who sought protection in the United States.[2] In the face of intransigence on the part of the executive branch,[3] Congress set out a refugee definition that complied with U.S. international legal obligations under the U.N. Refugee Convention and prescribed permanent,[4] equitable, and transparent procedures for the asylum process.[5] Over the next thirty-eight years, this commitment to protecting asylum seekers who had reached the United States' borders was upheld by Republican and Democratic administrations alike; though the asylum system was hardly perfect,[6] the executive branch was generally faithful to congressional intent as expressed in the 1980 act.[7]

Enter the Trump administration. Building on the foundation that Congress had established, prior administrations had constructed a functioning asylum system. But it was built from sticks, not bricks—and Trump blew the entire house down. Beginning in 2018, Trump and his attorneys general systematically demolished the system of humanitarian protections for asylum seekers, twisting statutory language beyond recognition through adjudicatory rulings, procedural changes, regulations of dubious legality, new fees, and even changes in forms and how they are processed. Congress's efforts in 1980 to ensure that the executive branch implemented an accurate refugee definition and a fair asylum process were simply no match for an administration hell-bent on their destruction. It had long been the case that "the inauguration of a new president can bring with it remarkable changes in immigration policy."[8] But the Trump administration rendered quaint the prior concerns about executive overreach and made mincemeat of checks and balances in the immigration arena.[9]

This book offers a comprehensive examination of the rise and demise of the U.S. asylum system. Starting with the United States' shameful failure to protect German Jews from the Holocaust, it explains the roots of Congress's interest in passing a statute that ensured that the executive branch would create a formal asylum system. This legislation would implement the United States' international legal obligations under the U.N. Refugee Convention, and it would put an end to ad hoc executive actions vis-à-vis refugee admissions, instead creating a transparent process that applied the substantive legal standards laid out in the treaty.

Chapter 1 of this book describes the Refugee Act of 1980, explaining both the substantive standards laid out by Congress and the process put in place by the executive branch. It walks the reader through each of the challenges faced by the asylum system in the decades after the signing of the act into law. Some of these problems were resolved by Democratic and Republican administrations alike, and others were created by the executive branch. Congress also made several changes to the asylum statute, including some that laid the seeds for the demolition of the asylum program. Chapter 2 explores the course of the asylum system under the Clinton, Bush, and Obama administrations.

In 2018, Trump began to destroy the asylum system in earnest. Chapters 3 through 5 comprehensively examine his administration's countless attacks on the asylum process. They begin with the efforts of his attorneys general to undermine substantive asylum law, some of which have been enjoined by the federal courts. Chapter 3 continues with the Trump administration's strikes on the asylum process; through changes small and large, his executive branch has systematically dismantled the affirmative asylum system and weakened the immigration courts. Chapter 4 analyzes the minefield of obstacles the Trump administration has created to block access to the asylum process, particularly for those requesting protection at the southern U.S. border. Chapter 5 describes the final nails in the coffin: the Trump administration's regulations that would end asylum altogether, and its subsequent measures to pile on even more restrictions.

Yet all is not lost. Chapter 6 envisions the possibility of a new beginning and the reconstruction of an even stronger asylum system. The Biden administration can and should quickly fix many of the changes made by the Trump executive branch. The first part of chapter 6 describes three methods through which it can undo some of its predecessor's wreckage. The Biden administration should immediately terminate programs that are not mandated by any law or regulation, such as the "Migrant Protection Protocols," which have exiled many asylum seekers to Mexico, and it should change forms and policies that are not required by Trump-era regulations. A new attorney general should reverse decisions by attorneys general Sessions and Barr that restricted asylum for victims of domestic violence and others. The Biden team should also revise or repeal several of the Trump administration's regulations that upended years of settled law and policy to put new obstacles in the path of legitimate asylum seekers—although, as the text explains, the process of putting new regulations into force can sometimes take years. More quickly and most important, it can settle more than a dozen lawsuits that have been filed against Trump regulations and policies, and it can withdraw Trump-initiated appeals of court orders that have enjoined Trump's restrictions.

In the long run, however, Congress should act to restore and improve America's asylum system. Having seen the destruction the Trump administration wrought on the Refugee Act of 1980, it is now time for Congress to "counteract the ambition" of the other political branch.[10] The system of checks and balances so carefully designed by the founders did not intend the executive branch to run roughshod over congressional intent. Congress must put in place robust checks that are more resistant to executive intransigence than its initial attempt to do so through the Refugee Act.[11] It should do so by legislating with precision, using what is known as ex ante controls,[12] in order to limit administrative discretion in the execution of the law.[13] Given that asylum seekers do not have any direct voice, and only a limited indirect voice, in the political process, statutory specificity is particularly important to protect their interests.[14] "Congressional specificity [also] facilitates judicial control," enabling the courts to ensure that the executive is faithfully executing the laws as Congress intended.[15] Finally, legislating with specificity is more beneficial for the nation's democracy because the legislative process is far more transparent than administrative lawmaking.[16] The political polarization of the national legislature and its lack of expertise in asylum law pose a serious challenge to a congressional fix.[17] Executive branch reforms, however, could be reversed by another subsequent administration hostile to immigration or asylum. To avoid this outcome, Congress should reform the statute to convert the U.S. asylum system into a brick house that cannot again be dismantled.

The Refugee Protection Act, which has been proposed in several sessions of Congress by Senator Patrick Leahy and Representative Zoe Lofgren, contains many thoughtful suggestions to rebuild the asylum system. But the Leahy and Lofgren bills were last revised in November 2019, and the Trump administration imposed a mountain of new restrictions in its last months, weeks, and days in office, as detailed in chapter 5. The second part of chapter 6 includes recommendations to Congress for creating a bill that would construct an effective bulwark against overreach by a future president who makes the exclusion of immigrants and refugees a central feature of executive branch policy.

This book was completed on January 20, 2021, as President Biden was taking the oath of office, having suggested that in his administration, the United States would again welcome refugees and asylum seekers. We hope that this book will both inform readers about the fragility of our nation's system of protection and help to guide Congress and administration officials in their efforts to make it robust.

1

THE REFUGEE ACT OF 1980

The Holocaust as Prologue

The Refugee Act of 1980—the foundation of America's asylum law—was a response to the failure of the United States and other nations to rescue people targeted by the racial and political policies of Hitler's Third Reich. While the Nazis persecuted Jews, other minorities, LGBTQ+ persons, and political opponents, the United States had no laws in place to allow the executive branch to rescue victims of persecution, and Congress failed to enact new legislation to save them.

From 1933 to 1941, Hitler sought to "cleanse" Germany of its Jewish population. His strategy was to make their lives so unbearable that they would have no choice but to leave.[1] Within five years, one in four German Jews had escaped. In March 1938, Germany annexed Austria, which was home to nearly 200,000 Jews. Four months later, in July 1938, thirty-two nations held a nine-day conference in the French resort town of Evian to consider a rescue plan. Most of these nations, including the United States, refused to take in German and Austrian Jews, many of whom perished in the Holocaust.[2]

U.S. federal law enacted in 1924 severely restricted immigration, establishing quotas for visas from European nations. Due to anti-Semitism at the State Department, 60 percent of the visa quota for Germans went unused in the prewar years.[3] In 1939, President Franklin D. Roosevelt refused to allow the *St. Louis*, a ship carrying over 900 Jewish refugees from Germany, to dock in Miami. As a result, the ship was forced to return to Europe, where half the passengers perished in the Holocaust.[4]

The vast majority of those targeted because of their race, nationality, religion, sexual orientation, or political opposition could not find refuge abroad. The Nazis murdered many millions of European civilians in death camps. Photographs of murdered Jews and emaciated survivors in camps liberated by the Allied armies toward the end of World War II vividly exposed these horrors.

The United Nations Refugee Convention

The failure of the international community to rescue refugees, together with the emergence of Cold War refugees, provoked the creation of an international treaty to protect certain people who fled individualized harm. More than 1 million European refugees displaced during World War II refused to return to countries where they had fled mortal threats and other forms of persecution.[5] In addition, new refugees began to escape to Western Europe once the Soviet Union asserted control over Eastern European states.

The 1951 Refugee Convention,[6] which was among the first human rights treaties of the modern era created by the international community, filled in an important gap in international law, enabling those with a well-founded fear of persecution to rebuild their lives in a country of refuge.[7] The treaty focused on protecting refugees from persecution based on their fundamental characteristics and beliefs: religion, race, nationality, political opinion, and membership in a particular social group.[8] At its core, the treaty substituted the protection of a new host government for that of a government that was unwilling or unable to protect certain citizens and residents. The treaty promised both humanitarian protection and, by connecting refugees to a nation, international stability.

However, the Refugee Convention protected only refugees who fled events that occurred before 1951 and allowed for an optional geographical limitation to Europe. As significant numbers of displaced people crossed borders seeking safety amid anticolonial conflict and civil wars in the 1950s and 1960s, the international community globalized the refugee definition. In 1967, it added the Refugee Protocol, removing the treaty's temporal and optional geographic restrictions.[9] Although the United States had not signed the 1951 treaty, it did accede to the protocol, which incorporated by reference the terms of the Refugee Convention.

The Indochinese Refugee Crisis

The United States' withdrawal of troops from Vietnam in 1975 left many Indochinese nationals who had assisted America and its allies during the conflict with no choice but to escape for their safety. Hundreds of thousands attempted to flee Indochina by boat to Malaysia, the Philippines, Singapore, Indonesia, and Hong Kong. Large numbers also crossed the land borders into Thailand and China.[10]

Four years after withdrawing from the Indochinese war, the United States headed the rescue program for refugees associated with the United States–led war effort. In his July 1979 appeal at the UN Conference on Indochinese Refugees in Geneva, Vice President Walter Mondale explained that though the United States had already welcomed over 200,000 Indochinese and planned on welcoming another 168,000 refugees in the coming year, and the nations that belonged to the Association of Southeast Asian Nations, China, and Hong Kong had offered safety and asylum to over half a million refugees, the international community could not keep up with the growing exodus. This is how Mondale appealed to European and other nations to accept refugees:

"The boat people." "The land people." The phrases are new, but unfortunately their precedent in the annals of shame is not. Forty-one years ago this very week, another international conference on Lake Geneva concluded its deliberations. Thirty-two "nations of asylum" convened at Evian to save the doomed Jews of Nazi Germany and Austria. On the eve of the conference, Hitler flung the challenge in the world's face. He said, "I can only hope that the other world, which has such deep sympathy for these criminals, will at least be generous enough to convert the sympathy into practical aid."[11]

As the Office of the United Nations High Commissioner for Refugees reports, the United States led a successful international effort to rescue these refugees and avoid a greater humanitarian crisis.[12] Sympathetic to the plight of the Indochinese and cognizant of the importance to the international order of regularized refugee admissions, Congress turned its attention to domestic implementation of the refugee treaty that it had ratified in 1968.

Even though the United States helped negotiate the 1951 Refugee Convention and played a major international leadership role in rescuing refugees, congressional statutes defined refugees as only those fleeing communist persecution.[13] The Refugee Convention had set out a much broader definition of the term "refugee," encompassing people targeted for persecution because of an enumerated characteristic (race, nationality), a similarly fundamental trait (particular social group), or the victim's exercise of a core human right (religion, political opinion). Twelve years after the United States became a party to the protocol, Congress enacted the Refugee Act of 1980 to implement the promise of the convention through domestic law.[14] Importantly, the statute's definition of a refugee mirrored the convention definition.

At that time, the major humanitarian focus of the U.S. government concerned the rescue of tens of thousands of refugees from abroad—particularly the Indochinese, as discussed above.[15] Through the Refugee Act of 1980, Congress authorized the admission of such refugees identified by the State Department abroad by creating a consultation process with the executive branch and appropriating funds to help integrate the uprooted into American society. Until the Trump administration restricted the admission of refugees through both travel bans and significantly reduced resettlement, the United States' resettlement program was by far the most generous in the world, protecting some 3 million refugees and offering them a path to citizenship.[16]

In the 1970s, most refugees were identified while still abroad and resettled at government expense by the Department of State. But some people who fled persecution arrived in the United States on their own and asked for asylum. Although the Immigration and Naturalization Service (INS) preferred as much discretion as possible in determining which of these arrivals were refugees, Congress voted for a statutory asylum provision that assured due process protections: "Because the politicized nature of executive practice in the asylum area concerned Congress, some members supported statutory asylum procedures in order to assure the extension of the asylum remedy to those fleeing persecution from noncommunist countries."[17]

Accordingly, a provision of the Refugee Act of 1980 instructed the attorney general to establish a procedure to assess applications for protection by such asylum seekers.[18] A decade later, the INS created an Asylum Office and began highly professionalized training of the new Asylum Corps officers. As described more fully below, these officers make the initial asylum decisions for "affirmative" asylum applicants, people who have not been apprehended by immigration authorities but voluntarily come forward after arriving in the United States and ask the government for protection. In 1983, the attorney general also established the Executive Office for Immigration Review, creating procedures for Department of Justice attorneys called immigration judges to adjudicate asylum claims for individuals placed in deportation (now called removal) proceedings (described more fully below).

Judicial Constraints on Executive Politicization

If an asylum seeker successfully demonstrates that she meets the refugee definition and is not barred from admission for other reasons, the United States grants her asylum, which places her on a path to citizenship. Two major legal issues arose during the first decade of implementation: how much proof is required to be recognized as a refugee, and the extent to which U.S. politics and foreign affairs could affect who would be so classified.

The 1980 Refugee Act authorized the attorney general, who oversaw the INS at the time, to grant asylum on a discretionary basis to those who demonstrated a well-founded fear of persecution under the new refugee definition. The act also made it mandatory that the attorney general "withhold deportation" for those who "would" face persecution if returned to their home country. Congress did not define "well-founded fear" of persecution, but the Supreme Court did in a pair of decisions examining the standards of proof for asylum and the withholding of deportation (now called withholding of removal). In the *Stevic* case, the Court held that noncitizens seeking to avoid deportation must show a "clear probability" that they would be persecuted if returned to their native land.[19] In other words, a person seeking "withholding" had to prove eligibility under a "more probable than not" standard. Just three years later, in *Cardoza-Fonseca*, the Court decided that the standard for withholding of removal set out in *Stevic* was too high for asylum.[20] Instead, the Court suggested that asylum applicants can meet the "well-founded fear" standard if they can show a one in ten chance that they will be persecuted if returned to their home country.[21]

The arrival of thousands of Salvadoran and Guatemalan asylum seekers fleeing civil wars in the 1980s, at a time when the U.S. government supported authoritarian regimes in those countries and opposed leftist rebels, tested the new definition of a refugee. The Reagan administration refused to recognize that the governments of those countries produced refugees. Reagan officials called the asylum seekers "economic migrants" and granted asylum to hardly any of them.[22] As the first director of the Asylum Office observed,

> Cold War policies often conflicted with the nonideological definition of refugee contained in the 1951 United Nations Convention as adopted by the United States in 1980. Adoption of that definition implied that concerns about foreign policy and immigration control should not enter into domestic asylum eligibility determinations and that the United States must offer asylum to all people with well-founded fears of certain kinds of persecution, regardless if the persecution be at the hands of friends of the United States or foes.[23]

Members of Congress and advocates for refugee protection criticized the INS for politicizing the treatment of asylum seekers. In 1985, a coalition of religious and refugee assistance organizations filed a lawsuit to challenge the discriminatory treatment of these asylum seekers. The Bush administration ultimately settled the case, *American Baptist Churches v. Thornburgh*, in early 1991. The settlement allowed many Salvadorans and Guatemalans another opportunity to assert their asylum claims.[24]

The Asylum Adjudicators

After ten years of implementing the Refugee Act of 1980 in a political manner that reflected the conservative orientation of the Reagan and Bush administrations, the INS promulgated a final asylum rule.[25] Pursuant to this new rule, the INS established a corps of professional asylum officers trained in refugee law and human rights conditions and gave them access to information about human rights violations worldwide.[26] These adjudicators assess the claims of the affirmative asylum applicants (i.e., those who come forward voluntarily to apply).

The INS created this professional group of adjudicators for its Asylum Office to depoliticize the implementation of asylum law. The INS purposely separated asylum officers from all other offices assessing immigration applications or enforcing immigration laws. As David Martin, a former INS general counsel, explained, "Traditionally, affirmative asylum claims were handled by journeyman examiners in the INS district offices."[27] However, according to Martin, adjudicating asylum claims may be "the most ambitious and challenging adjudication known to our administrative law":

> High stakes ride on the outcome: a secure status in a stable country versus, at best, return to an impoverished and troubled country (for most applicants), and at worst, deportation to a homeland where persecution awaits. The deciding officer or judge must determine what happened in the past in a distant country, based on a deeply imperfect factual record. The only available witness to the crucial individual facts is usually the applicant herself. She may, on the one hand, have reason to exaggerate past abuses or threats in order to gain a favorable ruling. Or she may be so distraught over past treatment or so fearful

of any authority figure that she cannot give a convincing account of her travails.[28]

In light of the humanitarian nature of asylum, the Asylum Office designed a nonadversarial process. After reviewing an affirmative application, an asylum officer interviews the asylum seeker to understand the nature of the claim, assesses credibility, and determines whether the individual has demonstrated a well-founded fear of persecution and meets all other statutory requirements. The officer's role is inquisitorial—no representative for the government is assigned to oppose the grant of asylum, and asylum seekers may be represented by counsel at their own expense.[29] In the first years of the new Asylum Office, the adjudicators either granted or denied asylum based on the interview and any documentary evidence.

Those apprehended by immigration authorities and summoned to deportation hearings could also seek asylum in "defensive" applications; but under the immigration law, their claims were heard by the officials presiding over those hearings rather than by asylum officers. Three years after the Refugee Act of 1980 became law, immigration judges at the new Executive Office for Immigration Review in the Department of Justice began to adjudicate defensive asylum claims.[30] Unlike federal court judges, the immigration judges are not independent of the executive branch. They are attorneys appointed by the attorney general and are "the attorney general's delegates in the cases that come before them."[31]

Immigration court hearings are adversarial. The government is represented by a prosecuting attorney whose role is to cross-examine the applicant and argue (for the most part) why asylum is not warranted.[32] An asylum applicant who can afford an attorney or obtain the services of pro bono counsel may be represented at the trial.[33] If the asylum seeker presents credible testimony and, if available, evidence establishing a well-founded fear of persecution, and meets all the statutory requirements, the immigration judge may grant asylum. In principle, even an individual who establishes eligibility for asylum can be denied it as a matter of discretion based on behavior that the immigration judge determines to reflect badly on the applicant's character, such as failure to pay U.S. income taxes.[34] But case law frowned on such denials, and historically, they have been rare.[35] If the immigration judge determines that the applicant should not be granted asylum and is ineligible for withholding of removal or other relief, the judge issues an order of deportation (now called a removal order).[36]

The First Asylum Crisis and the 1994 Reforms

In the early 1990s, the INS hired roughly 150 asylum officers to adjudicate affirmative claims.[37] But for several reasons, the caseload quickly overwhelmed the Asylum Corps. First, a significant number of applicants submitted claims largely to obtain temporary work authorization rather than because they actually feared persecution. The 1986 Immigration Reform and Control Act required noncitizens to demonstrate their eligibility for employment to employers, so many undocumented immigrants applied for asylum to obtain an Employment Authorization Document (EAD). In the early 1990s, asylum seekers could receive an EAD three months after they submitted an affirmative asylum claim. Asylum officers had to adjudicate the EAD applications as well as the asylum claims. Second, large numbers of Salvadorans and Guatemalans became eligible to reapply for asylum in 1991 pursuant to the settlement of the abovementioned *American Baptist Churches* case.[38] Finally, many officers were sent to Guantánamo Naval Base to screen thousands of Haitians whom the U.S. Coast Guard had interdicted in the international waters off the coast of Haiti as they headed toward the United States and had then brought to Guantánamo. As the INS noted, "By 1993, the asylum system was in a crisis, having become a magnet for abuse by persons filing applications in order to obtain employment authorization. As a result, most claims languished in the backlog for years, without being processed. By the end of fiscal year (FY) 1994, there were almost 425,000 cases in the backlog, nearly double what it had been two years earlier."[39]

This rising backlog threatened to overwhelm the system and make it impossible for legitimate claims to be assessed. Some asylum seekers were detained until the government could decide whether their protection claims were valid. But the INS was able to detain only a fraction of them. The New York District director of the INS, William Slattery, complained that more than 10,000 foreign nationals arrived at John F. Kennedy Airport each year and claimed asylum but that he could not detain them until their claims could be adjudicated because he did not control enough jail space.[40]

Slattery amplified his complaint by pointing to two terrorist attacks committed by people in the queue for asylum adjudication, and the revelation of a failed smuggling operation in 1993. One of the terrorist attacks was the shooting of five Central Intelligence Agency employees in the parking lot of their headquarters; the other was the explosion of a bomb in the garage of the World Trade Center that killed six people. The third event was the grounding of a ship carrying 286 Chinese passengers being smuggled into the United States in waters near New York City. Ten died trying to reach shore; most of the rest were sent to jails from which they applied for asylum.[41]

In the midst of national publicity about these events, Slattery went very public with his complaint, giving interviews to several magazines and newspapers and finally appearing in a much-watched segment of CBS's *Sixty Minutes.* He claimed that "the aliens have taken control. The third world has packed its bags and it's moving."[42] His proposed solution was not to expand the INS's capacity to hear cases, or even to increase the amount of jail space so that more asylum seekers could be detained. Instead, he advocated that those arriving by air be given a quick screening interview, in the airport, and then turned around on the next plane if they could not establish a good case for asylum.

The INS consulted widely with advocates, government officials, and other stakeholders.[43] Rather than asking Congress to change the law as Slattery requested, it issued a final rule, effective on January 4, 1995, to solve the backlog and related problems.[44]

To address concerns about work authorization, the INS instituted constraints on access to work permits. Under the reforms, asylum seekers became eligible to apply for employment authorization only after asylum was granted or 150 days after the date of filing if a decision had not been made.[45]

The reforms also ensured that asylum seekers who lost at the asylum office would face deportation proceedings. Before submitting applications pursuant to the reformed procedures, all affirmative asylum seekers were informed that unsuccessful applications would be referred directly to the immigration court for a deportation hearing if the applicants did not have other legal status, as was true for most.[46] Under the changes, applicants risked receiving a removal order if they could not persuade either the asylum officer or the immigration judge that they qualified as refugees.

To ensure timely decisions, the Asylum Office hired and trained a substantial number of new corps members. The number of asylum officers increased from 150 to 325, and the number of immigration judges from 112 to 179.[47] To demonstrate that asylum officers could adjudicate new cases in a timely manner, the INS created a last in / first out decision-making system, whereby backlog cases would be reached only after the Asylum Office demonstrated that it could keep up with the new incoming caseload. The INS did not want to create new incentives for claims to be filed by those solely interested in work permits (which, under the new system, became available if a case was not adjudicated in a timely fashion).

The Asylum Office reforms were successful; as the INS noted, "Asylum reform has led to a decrease of 75 percent in the number of new claims being filed with the INS.... Conversely, the approval rate of cases heard by INS asylum officers has increased from 15 percent of cases adjudicated in FY 1993 to an approval rate of 38 percent in FY 1999, another indicator that the INS is receiving more valid claims."[48]

These higher approval rates demonstrated that the reformed system had largely eliminated the problems created by applicants solely seeking work authorization. Not only did asylum officers keep up with incoming applications; ultimately, they eliminated the backlog. Moreover, the Asylum Office ensured that refugees were able to avail themselves of the protections set out in the Refugee Act of 1980 in a timely manner.

The INS Gender Guidelines

In the 1990s, the INS decided to develop guidelines to assist asylum officers to more fully address the protection needs of female asylum seekers. The agency leadership consulted widely with interested governmental and nongovernmental experts, as well as with the Office of the United Nations High Commissioner for Refugees, to develop guidelines that addressed both substantive and procedural issues that may arise when interviewing women and assessing their claims.[49]

During this formative period of asylum adjudication in the United States, asylum officers had to determine the extent to which various forms of serious harm suffered by women are covered by the refugee definition. This persecution ranged from rape and female genital mutilation to being stoned or burnt to death for not bringing enough dowry. In 1995, the INS produced guidelines that addressed the seriousness of the harm, including sexual violence; the nexus of that persecution to actual or imputed political opinion as well as to membership in a particular social group defined by gender and by family membership; the role of the government as persecutor or as unable or unwilling to control the persecutor; and the availability of protection elsewhere in the home country.[50]

FROM CLINTON TO OBAMA

The Illegal Immigration Reform and Immigrant Responsibility Act of 1996

In the election of 1994, Republican majorities, running on the conservative platform of the "Contract with America," swept into office in both the House and the Senate. The new legislative leaders did not care whether the reforms that the Immigration and Naturalization Service (INS) had recently instituted were successful. With President Clinton's acquiescence, they enacted the Illegal Immigration Reform and Immigrant Responsibility Act of 1996 (IIRIRA),[1] which made sweeping changes in the immigration laws, including five new restrictions affecting asylum applicants.[2]

The first of the new restrictions was a prohibition on asylum for anyone who did not file an application within a year of entering the United States, with only two narrow exceptions.[3] Neither exception explicitly included a lack of knowledge that the United States had a system for offering asylum or a lack of knowledge of the filing deadline.[4]

The second new restriction, similar to the airport interviews that Slattery advocated (as described in chapter 1), created a hurdle for many asylum seekers called "expedited removal," which would become a major obstacle to protection during the Trump administration. Foreign nationals who arrived in the United States without required visas would be asked by border agents whether they were afraid to return to their own countries. The border agents were instructed not to mention the word "asylum." Those who did not express a fear would be promptly deported with no further procedure. Those who expressed fear would be given screening interviews by asylum officers to determine whether their stories were credible and whether, if those stories were true, the migrants could qualify for asylum based on the statutory standard. If they passed the "credible fear" screening test, they would be given a chance to prove to an immigration judge that they qualified for asylum, though, at the INS's discretion, they could be jailed for months until a hearing was held. If they failed the screening test, prompt deportation would follow. Asylum seekers subject to this screening procedure were not allowed to be represented by counsel during the interview, though if they were lucky enough to have attorneys, the lawyers could counsel them before the interview to help them understand what aspects of their histories were relevant to the decision.[5] Migrants who were barred by statute from receiving asylum (e.g., those who had previously been deported) might later be granted withholding of removal by an immigration judge.[6] The asylum officer would screen those individuals using a stricter "reasonable fear" standard, and, like those who failed to demonstrate credible fear, those who failed this test were immediately deported.

The gatekeeping by border officials was a significant obstacle along the way to a possible day in court because officials often failed to ask the questions about fear of return that they had been instructed to ask.[7] But until late 2019, a majority of those who made it to the second stage of the process—the credible fear screening—were eventually granted full immigration court hearings on their asylum claims because the asylum officers determined in most cases that they passed the credible fear test.[8]

During the Clinton administration, the new procedure was applied only to asylum seekers who arrived in the United States by air or at the land ports of entry. But Congress had given the government discretion to apply it more broadly, and the George W. Bush administration expanded expedited removal so that it would apply to those who arrived by sea and, more significantly, to those who were apprehended within 100 miles of the Mexican border within two weeks after they had entered.[9] As we shall see, the Bush administration's expansion meant that in later years, tens of thousands of Central Americans fleeing from violence in that region would be subjected to expedited removal. During the Trump administration, many would be deported without full hearings on their applications.

The third restriction prohibited the government from granting asylum to an applicant who could be removed to a "safe third country."[10] Congress limited this bar in several ways. It applied only if the country to which the government wanted to deport the asylum seeker was in fact "safe," which Congress defined as a nation where the person's life or freedom would not be threatened on one of the grounds for which the Refugee Act afforded protection and which had a "full and fair procedure" for determining a claim to asylum. Moreover, to qualify a third country as "safe," the United States had to have entered into an agreement with that country providing for such deportations.

When IIRIRA was enacted, no such agreements existed. The Bush administration did enter into such an agreement with Canada in 2004, but it had only a limited effect.[11] It barred migrants crossing from the United States into Canada at Canada's land ports of entry from seeking asylum in Canada, but it did not apply to those who traveled by air into Canada or who crossed into Canada on foot through the woods rather than at a border-crossing post. The real importance of the safe third-country bar was not apparent until 2019, when the Trump administration entered into deportation agreements with the countries of the Northern Triangle of Central

America—El Salvador, Guatemala, and Honduras—after alleging that they were "safe."[12]

The fourth restriction was a limitation on asylum seekers' ability to seek judicial review. Congress barred the federal courts from hearing appeals from asylum applicants who did not pass the credible fear screening test.[13] It also prohibited the federal courts from reviewing most determinations that an applicant had missed the one-year application deadline or failed to qualify for an exception to the deadline.[14] In addition, it permitted only one lawsuit to challenge the constitutionality of the expedited removal procedures and required that if one were filed, it could only be filed within sixty days after the law was implemented and could only be brought in the federal court for the District of Columbia.[15]

The fifth restriction, like the third, was one that lay dormant for twenty-two years until brought to life by the Trump administration. Congress wanted to prevent migrants with criminal convictions from staying in the United States pending their removal hearing. This provision therefore permitted the government to "return" to Mexico certain migrants arriving across the border from that country to await their Immigration Court hearings.[16] The Trump administration's interpretation of this statutory provision to push back asylum seekers into dangerous Mexican border towns was unprecedented, as further discussed in chapter 4.[17]

Finally, the 1996 immigration law provides that pending a final decision on credible fear, an applicant in the expedited removal process "shall be detained." (Although the law also permits the detention of all undocumented asylum seekers while they are awaiting court hearings,[18] the government has only very rarely detained those who entered the United States with visas and came forward to apply for asylum affirmatively, even if they fell out of legal status before the government made final decisions in their cases.)[19] The Department of Homeland

Security (DHS) routinely detains asylum seekers without proper documents who are apprehended at or near the border while they await removal proceedings, whether or not they present themselves at an official port of entry.[20]

Two provisions of the law allowed the government to release from detention certain asylum seekers (including those subjected to credible fear screening). Those who had entered the United States between ports of entry[21] could be released on payment of a money bond,[22] although officials often set the bond amount so high that the funds could not be raised even with the assistance of a friend or relative.[23] All asylum seekers could be released on "parole," but such release was entirely in the discretion of Immigration and Customs Enforcement (ICE) officials, and it could be denied altogether, resulting in long periods of incarceration, or it could be conditioned on agreement by the asylum seeker to wear an ankle monitor at all times and to report as often as directed to an ICE official.[24]

As William Slattery noted in the mid-1990s, only a small fraction of undocumented migrants, including asylum seekers, were detained before the enactment of IIRIRA. As the government detained more immigrants, ICE rented space in county jails and offered contracts to the burgeoning private prison industry, which opened thirteen "immigrant-only" prisons.[25] Immigration detention contracts were so lucrative that they saved the two largest and most prominent private prison companies from financial ruin.[26] Congress exacerbated the problem in 2009, passing an appropriations rider that required ICE to have 34,000 beds available at all times for immigration detainees,[27] which ICE interpreted as requiring it to keep 34,000 people in detention at all times.[28]

The Homeland Security Act of 2002

The Homeland Security Act of 2002, which created DHS, changed the structure of the government's institutions that adjudicate asylum claims. The INS was dissolved. In its place, three different DHS agencies were given duties that involve interacting with asylum seekers. The Asylum Office, which adjudicates affirmative applications and conducts credible fear interviews for those put into expedited removal, was assigned to U.S. Citizenship and Immigration Services (USCIS), known as the benefits arm of the agency. Customs and Border Protection (CBP) was created to inspect the credentials of people entering at legal land, sea, and air ports of entry into the United States and to apprehend individuals who tried to enter without presenting themselves for inspection at these official crossing points. The third agency, Immigration and Customs Enforcement, is responsible for detaining migrants who are not lawfully present, including asylum seekers who have been apprehended by CBP or by ICE officials, and for deporting migrants subject to a final order of removal. ICE trial attorneys also usually oppose asylum claims in immigration court. The Department of Justice, in which the INS had been located, retained the fourth agency that interacts with asylum seekers, the Executive Office for Immigration Review, which continues to house the immigration courts and the Board of Immigration Appeals.

The REAL ID Act of 2005

The 2002 restructuring legislation did not change the standards for granting asylum; three years later, Congress returned to the subject. The main purpose of the 2005 REAL ID Act was to impose tighter security standards for state-issued forms of identification such as drivers' licenses, which could be used to board domestic airline flights. But three new provisions buried in the act had implications for asylum seekers.

The first of the new provisions authorized adjudicators to justify a denial of asylum on the ground that the applicant was not credible on the basis of any of several factors, such as demeanor; responsiveness; inconsistency with prior statements, even if not made under oath; or inaccuracies "without regard to whether [they go] to the heart of the applicant's claim."[29]

The REAL ID Act also changed the corroboration standards. The new law authorized an adjudicator to deny asylum if the applicant failed to provide corroborating evidence (e.g., sworn eyewitness statements, medical records, or arrest warrants) to supplement otherwise credible testimony, "unless the applicant does not have the evidence and cannot reasonably obtain the evidence."[30] The act specified that whether or not evidence was reasonably obtainable was a question of fact rather than law, which meant that appellate courts were required to examine an immigration judge's negative decision under a deferential standard of review.[31]

The third change codified a more restrictive standard for "mixed motive" cases, which would apply, for example, to a migrant who had come to the United States both to flee a persecutor and to escape from dire poverty. Some prior cases had held that asylum could be granted if flight from persecution was one of several motives for travel to the United States.[32] The act sought to limit the discretion of adjudicators by specifying that a well-founded fear of persecution had to be "at least one central reason" for the migration.[33]

The Bush Administration

In 2005, the number of Central Americans arrested near the Mexican border more than doubled.[34] These migrants were fleeing extraordinary levels of gang violence; El Salvador, Guatemala, and Honduras faced the highest homicide rates in the world of any nations not at war.[35] The roots of this violence can be traced back to the civil wars in El Salvador and Guatemala in the late 1980s and early 1990s. Many Central American families fled the violence of the guerrillas and the state, seeking refuge in the United States. These refugee families often landed in gang-controlled neighborhoods, where the children learned to protect themselves by forming their own gangs, such as MS-13 and Calle-18, named after streets in Los Angeles.[36] IIRIRA had enabled the INS to deport noncitizens convicted of a wide variety of crimes, exporting gang violence to Central America. In 2005, Central American families were once again fleeing violence, this time at the hands of those gangs.[37]

President George W. Bush saw the expansion of immigration detention space—for asylum seekers, among others—as an opportunity to deter migration by jailing more migrants. Faced with an increasing number of Central American mothers and children who arrived together to seek refuge in the United States, the Bush administration contracted with the Corrections Corporation of America, one of the largest private prison companies, to incarcerate these families at a detention center in Texas, some for a year or more, while they awaited immigration court hearings.[38] Conditions in the T. Don Hutto Family Residential Center were horrific, provoking national publicity and a federal lawsuit that was eventually settled.[39] The settlement produced some improvements in the facility but no releases of the families.[40] The nation's first jail for migrant families continued in operation until 2009, when President Barack Obama shut it down.[41]

The Bush administration took two other actions that had significant impacts on asylum seekers. The first was to increase the rate at which the Board of Immigration Appeals (BIA) upheld denials of asylum claims. The administration took two steps to achieve this goal. First, it changed the procedural rules. For decades, an asylum denial could be upheld only by a three-member panel of the BIA imparting some degree of deliberation to the process. In 2002, the administration amended its procedures to enable individual members of the BIA to uphold denials of asylum and to do so without writing opinions explaining the reasoning underlying those denials.[42] This change made it easier to uphold a denial, though a decision to protect an asylum seeker in the face of an immigration court denial generally required a three-member panel to issue a written opinion. Second, the administration purged the BIA of the five members appointed by the prior Clinton administration, with whom it disagreed ideologically.[43] The combined result of these changes in procedure and personnel was that the rate at which the BIA reversed denials of asylum—in other words, found in favor of the asylum seeker—dropped dramatically. In fiscal year (FY) 2001, the BIA's reversal rate was 37 percent. By FY 2005, this rate had dropped to 11 percent.[44]

The third initiative of the Bush administration was to apply expedited removal to many more people, though this change would largely affect those who arrived during later administrations. IIRIRA allowed expedited removal procedures to be applied to those who arrived without visas at airports and seaports, but it also authorized the attorney general to expand the application of expedited removal. In 2004, the attorney general used this authority to begin to impose expedited removal screening on the "nearly 1 million" undocumented migrants apprehended annually within 100 miles of the southern border, unless they could prove they had already been in the United States for more than two weeks.[45] At first, this change had only a minor impact on those seeking asylum after crossing the Rio Grande, because during the Bush presidency, more than 80 percent of those who said they were afraid of returning home were certified by asylum officers to have a credible fear of persecution, enabling them to go on to present their claims to immigration judges.[46] But when the Trump administration later tightened the standards and procedures for passing the credible fear test, the expanded scope of expedited removal would become an important tool for deporting asylum applicants.[47]

The Obama Administration

After Obama took office, his administration took steps toward correcting some of the harsh policies that had been put into place in earlier years.[48] It closed Hutto as a family detention center. It unsuccessfully supported a comprehensive immigration reform bill that would have included a repeal of the one-year deadline for asylum applications.[49] And the Board of Immigration Appeals resolved an issue that had bedeviled immigration adjudicators for a decade, ruling that domestic violence victims could constitute a social group and could therefore be eligible for asylum.[50]

But in 2014, the administration took a tough stance on the humanitarian crisis in Central America. Between 2005 and 2014, violence in the Northern Triangle had escalated sharply. From 2005 to 2011, the reported homicide rate in Honduras more than doubled, growing from 41 to 85 per 100,000 inhabitants,[51] and by 2015, El Salvador had 104 homicides per 100,000 inhabitants.[52] These countries also suffered some of the world's highest rates of femicide—murders of women because of their gender.[53]

Before 2014, most migrants apprehended at the southern border were single male adults from Mexico. Starting in 2014, the demographics of that migrant population began to shift.[54] Many of the new border crossers were Central American children seeking protection, some traveling alone and others arriving with at least one parent. Apprehensions of non-Mexicans at the southern border increased from 46,997 individuals in FY 2011 to 148,988 in FY 2013 and to 252,600 in FY 2014.[55] Two striking changes involved children. The number of unaccompanied children who were apprehended jumped from 24,481 in FY 2012 to 68,451 in FY 2014,[56] and the number of apprehensions of family groups that included children increased by 361 percent in a single year, from FY 2013 to FY 2014.[57]

Like its predecessor, the Obama administration responded with a policy of deterrence by incarceration. President Obama had allocated his political capital to the expansion of Deferred Action for Childhood Arrivals and a new program for the undocumented parents of children born in the United States (i.e., Deferred Action for Parents of Americans and Lawful Permanent Residents) that he would announce before the midterm election. To demonstrate that he was not "soft" on immigration, Obama locked up increasing numbers of asylum seekers at the southern border.[58] In response to the influx of families, the Obama administration reversed course after having closed Hutto five years earlier. It first opened a temporary family detention center at a remote location in Artesia, New Mexico. When that center became insufficient to detain these families, the administration established two massive family detention centers near Karnes City and Dilley, Texas, both run by private prison companies.[59] It also unsuccessfully defended litigation challenging the long-term incarceration of children in those facilities.[60]

LEGAL RESTRICTIONS AND PROCEDURAL OBSTACLES IMPOSED BY THE TRUMP ADMINISTRATION

Donald J. Trump's hostility to immigrants was apparent as early as 2015, when he announced his intention to run for president. "When Mexico sends its people, they're not sending their best," he said. "They're sending people that have lots of problems, and they're bringing those problems with us. They're bringing drugs. They're bringing crime. They're rapists. And some, I assume, are good people."[1] In office, he made it clear that his antipathy extended worldwide and to refugees seeking protection in America. In 2018, at an Oval Office meeting with members of Congress devoted to protecting Central Americans, Haitians, and Africans, Trump asked, "Why are we having all these people from shithole countries come here?"[2]

Trump believed that he owed his election in large part to his voters' opposition to immigration.[3] To cater to his electoral base, he attacked both the letter and the spirit of the 1980 Refugee Act. In addition to slashing the number of refugees admitted annually through the auspices of the State Department,[4] he took aim at the asylum system, erecting many new obstacles, some of them seemingly insurmountable, in the path of people seeking American protection from persecution and torture.

The Trump administration created three different types of barriers to asylum: (1) changes to substantive asylum law, (2) procedural obstacles within the asylum adjudication process, and (3) barricades to accessing the asylum process. The first two of these restrictions are discussed in this chapter, and the third is explored in chapter 4. In June 2020, when it became apparent that Trump could very probably lose his reelection bid, he proposed a comprehensive new regulation to bind his successor and end asylum in America. He followed that rule with a profusion of regulatory and policy changes, piling limitation on limitation so that few if any people would be able to win asylum in the future, even after his presidency ended. The changes he made in the last months of 2020 and the first weeks of 2021 are discussed in chapter 5.

Restricting Asylum via the Substantive Law

In an effort to close the border to asylum seekers from Central America, the Trump administration took direct aim at case law that protected women escaping domestic violence, refugees fleeing violence at the hands of nonstate actors, and individuals facing persecution due to familial relationships. These changes upended substantive asylum law and demonstrated an astonishing disrespect for precedent. The seminal social group decision, *Matter of Acosta*, decided by the Board of Immigration Appeals (BIA) in 1985, held that "the shared characteristic [that defines a particular social group] might be an innate one such as sex, color, or kinship ties." Moreover, U.S. asylum law had long held that refugees could seek protection from persecution at the hands of nonstate actors. Attorneys general Sessions and Barr's efforts to restrict the substantive law of asylum relied on a provision in immigration regulations that allows the attorney general to refer to himself, for further review, any decision of the BIA.[5] This practice, rarely used until the Trump administration, enabled Trump's attorneys general to inject politics into asylum precedents.[6] Decisions by Sessions , Barr, and—in the waning hours of the Trump administration—acting Attorney General Rosen eviscerated the definition of membership in a particular social group, thereby foreclosing most Central American asylum claims.[7]

Domestic Violence and Gang Violence

In June 2018, Sessions attempted to upend the case law establishing that women fleeing domestic violence could be members of a particular social group. Snatching the *Matter of A-B-* case from the hands of the BIA and referring it to himself, Sessions claimed that "victims of private criminal activity" were not likely to meet the particularity and social distinction prongs of the social group definition.[8] He also overruled a 2014 BIA decision, *Matter of A-R-C-G-*, which held that "married women in Guatemala who are unable to leave their relationship" was a valid particular social group, asserting that the BIA did not adequately analyze these two elements of the social group definition.[9]

In the same decision, he distorted the standard for claiming persecution by nonstate actors. Until the Trump administration began to eviscerate asylum law, applicants needed simply to show that a persecutor who was not a government official was a person or group that their country's government was "unable or unwilling to control."[10] The U.S. Citizenship and Immigration Services' (USCIS's) own guidance to asylum officers specified that "the applicant is not required to show direct government involvement or complicity with the non-government actor."[11] Decisions of the BIA affirmed asylum grants where the persecution was caused by nonstate actors, such as rebel groups and anti-Semitic mobs, that the government was "unable or unwilling to control."[12] The *A-B-* decision changed this standard, claiming that applicants persecuted by a nonstate actor must show that "the government condoned the private actions or at least demonstrated a complete helplessness to protect the victims." Sessions overturned *A-R-C-G-*, and he reversed the BIA's grant of asylum to Ms. A-B-.

Six months later, the District Court for the District of Columbia enjoined asylum officers from applying these aspects of *A-B-* when screening asylum applicants for credible fear.[13] Judge Emmet Sullivan found that "a general rule that effectively bars the claims based on certain categories of persecutors (i.e., domestic abusers or gang members) or claims related to certain kinds of violence" is inconsistent with congressional intent to bring U.S. law into conformity with international refugee law, and therefore violates the statute. Moreover, the court found that "it was clear at the time that the Act was passed by Congress that the 'unwilling or unable' standard did not require a showing that the government 'condoned' persecution or was 'completely helpless' to prevent it."[14]

In July 2020, the U.S. Court of Appeals for the District of Columbia affirmed the relevant portions of this decision: "The INA nowhere defines 'particular social group.' But in a line of decisions beginning with *Matter of Acosta*, . . . the Board has long defined the term to mean 'a group of persons all of whom share a common, immutable characteristic,' one they 'either cannot change, or should not be required to change because it is fundamental to their individual identities or consciences.'"[15] This basic definition is well accepted by the courts.

Writing for the court, Judge Tatel further explained that "under long-standing administrative and judicial precedent, the term 'persecution,' undefined in the INA, encompasses harm inflicted by nonstate actors." He restored the "unable or unwilling to control" standard for persecution at the hands of such actors.[16] The court also held that Attorney General Sessions had improperly ruled that in credible fear interviews, asylum officers should apply the law of the federal circuit in which the interview took place rather than the circuit with the interpretation of law most favorable to the asylum applicant, who might travel to any part of the country before applying for asylum.

Not to be so easily outdone, the attorney general responded in September 2020 with *Matter of A-C-A-A-*.[17] In this bold decision, Barr stated that *Matter of A-B-* overruled *Matter of A-R-C-G-* and that "there has been disagreement among the court of appeals about whether gender-based groups may constitute a particular social group within the meaning of the INA."[18] Barr emphasized that *Matter of A-B-* found that "claims involving violence inflicted by nongovernmental actors" are unlikely to succeed because they fail to establish government inability or unwillingness to address the persecution.[19] Dismissing the persecution suffered by the applicant as based on "personal animus,"[20] the attorney general profoundly mischaracterized the Court of Appeals' decision in *Grace v. Barr* as a win for the administration, saying that the case "reversed a district court decision calling into question some aspects of *Matter of A-B-*."[21] Barr's *A-C-A-A-* decision also included a new procedural rule to make it easier for the BIA to overturn an immigration judge's grant of asylum.[22]

With less than a week left in Trump's presidency, after Attorney General Barr had resigned, acting Attorney General Rosen issued yet another decision in *Matter of A-B-*.[23] Relying yet again on the self-referral mechanism, Rosen reasserted Attorney General Sessions's claims that the "unable or unwilling" standard requires asylum seekers persecuted by private actors to prove that the government condoned that harm or "demonstrated a complete helplessness" to protect them from that harm. In an exceptionally aggressive stance for an administrative adjudicator inferior in authority to the federal judiciary, Rosen takes aim at the D.C. Circuit for striking down that standard. Rosen claims that governmental involvement is required to establish persecution in an asylum claim and that "the inability to eradicate private crime" does not therefore establish persecution. The decision emphasizes the option of internal relocation, a fairly ludicrous proposition in Ms. A-B-'s home country of El Salvador, which is approximately the size of New Jersey. Finally, Rosen interprets the "one central reason" nexus to require that the protected ground must be both a but-for cause of and play more than a minor role in provoking the persecution. In a second show of remarkable hubris, Rosen takes the Fourth Circuit, a federal appellate court, to task for defining the nexus more broadly.

Families as Social Groups

Finally, notwithstanding *Acosta*'s listing of "kinship ties" as qualifying for the social group standard, and Courts of Appeals' decisions holding that family ties can provide a basis for asylum and understanding family as a "prototypical example of a 'particular social group,"[24] Attorney General Barr declared that a family could not usually qualify as a social group unless the family was one that was prominent and therefore socially distinct in the applicant's country. Repeating the "private criminal activity" argument, he found that an applicant persecuted by a gang due to his membership in the immediate family of his father was not a member of a particular social group.[25] Cross-motions for summary judgment in a case challenging the validity of Barr's ruling are pending in federal district court.[26]

New Procedural Obstacles

These efforts to undercut the Refugee Act through attorney general opinions excluding certain types of persecution were only the beginning of the administration's war on asylum seekers. It accompanied these measures with changes in asylum procedures that would make achieving protection more difficult for both affirmative applicants who had never been in removal proceedings and for those who applied for asylum after officials of the Department of Homeland Security (DHS) had summoned them to court.

Restricting Affirmative Asylum

Individuals who have entered the United States lawfully or have not been apprehended by the DHS may voluntarily apply for asylum, make their presence known to DHS, and have their applications adjudicated in the first instance by DHS asylum officers rather than by immigration judges in adversarial removal hearings.[27] These are known as affirmative asylum seekers, and the Trump administration has placed three significant bureaucratic obstacles in their paths. These impediments include new requirements for completing application forms, the imposition of application fees, and new employment authorization restrictions. Affirmative asylum seekers, many of whom entered the United States legally, must now jump through technical hoop after technical hoop in order to obtain protection in the United States.[28]

New application rules. In October 2019, the USCIS website was updated to include a statement that it would reject asylum applications if *any* field is left blank in the ten-page Form 1-589, Application for Asylum.[29] Asylum lawyers began receiving many more technical rejections after this guidance was issued.[30] For example, USCIS began rejecting applications in which the applicants had left blank the field for a middle name, rather than writing "N/A," even when they had no middle name. In response to a class action lawsuit, USCIS agreed to pause this policy as of December 23, 2020, while the parties engaged in settlement negotiations.[31]

At about the same time, DHS proposed to amend the asylum application form to make it more difficult to complete and to make it less likely that applicants could win their cases. For example, for the first time, the proposed form requires applicants claiming protection on social group grounds to lay out that social group at the very outset of their case. The new form warns that "you will not be found to be a refugee or have it decided that your life or freedom would be threatened based on membership in a particular social group in any case unless you first articulate on the record, or provide a basis on the record for determining, the definition and boundaries of the alleged particular social group."[32] The term "social group" in the Refugee Act is a technical legal term, which has been interpreted in many different ways by various federal courts and agencies. Lawyers often need to submit lengthy explanations to immigration judges defining their clients' social groups under governing law. Unrepresented applicants, many of whom do not speak English well and hardly any of whom are familiar with the technicalities of U.S. asylum law, may find it impossible to define their social group at the outset of the application process.[33]

New employment restrictions. In June 2020, DHS issued a final rule governing the issuance of employment authorization documents (work permits) to asylum seekers. For twenty-five years, asylum applicants were issued work permits if, through no fault of the asylum seeker, the government failed to decide their applications within 180 days.[34] This new regulation made a variety of changes that severely restrict asylum seekers' abilities to work in order to feed, house, and clothe themselves and their families. Asylum seekers will now have to wait a full year before they can apply for a work permit.[35] Asylum seekers who enter the United States between official ports of entry and fail to present themselves to DHS within 48 hours of entry will now be barred from applying for work permits, as will asylum applicants who file their asylum claims more than one year after entry.[36] Even if they are ultimately granted asylum, these individuals may have to wait five years, rather than one year, to obtain work permits, because as of 2020, immigration courts had four- to five-year backlogs.[37] This rule is being challenged in two federal lawsuits, one filed in Maryland in July 2020 that has met with preliminary success and another filed in D.C. in December 2020.[38] In August 2020, USCIS altered its policy manual to require that applicants prove that they merit a favorable exercise of discretion in addition to meeting the basic eligibility standards, thereby imposing yet another hurdle before an asylum-seeking migrant can work.[39]

Application fees. Until 2020, no fee was required for filing an asylum application or, for those who are eligible, for an initial employment application. This policy made sense because refugees often flee to the United States with very limited funds, and many who make the arduous journey through unsafe countries are robbed or extorted along the way. Once they arrive, asylum seekers are not allowed to work for six months after filing their applications. In 2020, DHS complied with a demand from President Trump to impose a $50 fee for asylum applications and, for those asylum applicants who remained eligible to work despite the new employment restrictions, a $510 fee for applications for employment authorization.[40] Under this new rule, fee waivers for indigent applicants are not available.[41] In September 2020, the federal district court for the Northern District of California enjoined the rule.[42]

Gutting the Immigration Courts

Despite these and other efforts by the Trump administration to curb asylum, some asylum cases were still being heard in immigration courts. The Constitution, the Immigration and Nationality Act, and implementing regulations require that immigration courts fairly consider each case. Foreign nationals in removal hearings in immigration court have a right to notice of the time and place of the hearing,[43] to be represented by counsel (although indigents are not entitled to free attorneys),[44] to present written and oral evidence,[45] to cross-examine adverse witnesses,[46] to reach a decision based on the record,[47] and to appeal that decision to the BIA and then to a federal Court of Appeals.[48]

President Trump, however, believed that "the asylum

procedures are ridiculous."[49] When he took office, the immigration courts had a backlog of more than 500,000 cases.[50] The president's solution was that "we have to do something about asylum. And to be honest with you, you have to get rid of judges."[51] In a 2018 tweet, Trump advocated denying asylum seekers any process at all: "We cannot allow all of these people to invade our Country. When somebody comes in, we must immediately, with no Judges or Court Cases, bring them back from where they came. Our system is a mockery to good immigration policy and Law and Order."[52]

The Metrics

The Trump administration took several steps to make it more difficult for judges to manage their dockets and consequently for asylum applicants to win relief in immigration court. It changed the performance standards by which the immigration judges would in the future be evaluated for promotion or possible transfer to less desirable locations.[53] For the first time, judges began to be evaluated based on the speed with which they adjudicated cases, which would almost certainly result in less time spent on each case. This meant, for example, that judges had less time to hear oral testimony, which is particularly important for unrepresented applicants who have little understanding of which facts are relevant to an asylum claim. A fair hearing in a well-prepared asylum case requires the judge to read many sworn declarations and other documents submitted by an applicant, and the oral hearing takes about three hours. More time is required if the judge has to write an opinion. But the new metrics provided that to earn a "satisfactory" rating a judge must resolve at least 700 cases a year.[54] The administrators of the court system track case completion figures, displaying individualized metrics to each judge on a digital "performance dashboard."[55]

Judge Amiena Khan, the vice president of the National Association of Immigration Judges,[56] observed that the metrics "seem like an attempt to turn judges from neutral arbiters into law enforcement agents enacting Trump administration policies."[57] Judge Ashley Tabaddor, the association's president, explained that these policies turn the immigration courts into "assembly line justice."[58] At about the same time, the administration took several other measures to increase the rate of removal orders. It eliminated the judges' ability to suspend or end cases where the applicant might receive legal immigration status from DHS, for reasons unrelated to asylum.[59] The administration even restricted the authority of judges to postpone hearing dates to provide more time for DHS to consider pending applications for legal status other than asylum.[60] These measures further limited the amount of time that judges could devote to the more complicated asylum cases.

Summary Judgments against Asylum Seekers

Until the Trump administration took office, every asylum seeker had a day in court. Neither the statute nor the regulations provide for summary judgment against an asylum seeker, except that an asylum applicant who does not appear in the courtroom after receiving notice may be ordered removed in absentia. In 2014, the BIA issued a nationwide precedent confirming asylum seekers' rights to testify in full hearings. A Honduran national had submitted an asylum application alleging that he was threatened with death because he was a member of a family that owned property. Several other family members had been murdered, and he himself had been shot at. The immigration judge dismissed the case without holding a hearing because, in his opinion, membership in a family did not qualify as membership in a particular social group. The BIA reversed,[61] holding that a judge could not dismiss an asylum claim without holding a hearing at which the immigrant could present oral evidence.[62] The decision was important because a pro se asylum applicant may not be adept at presenting a prima facie case on paper.[63] Questioning by an Immigration and Customs Enforcement (ICE) lawyer and by the judge may bring out facts that bolster the case for asylum.

That is where matters stood for four years, until, once again invoking self-referral authority, Attorney General Sessions suddenly plucked the case from the ether and vacated it as a precedent for future cases.[64] Legal observers were puzzled as to the attorney general's motives, as the technical basis for his short ruling was that the decision was moot. But many worried that it was laying the groundwork for a future attempt to eliminate hearings for asylum seekers.[65]

Law Enforcers as Judges

In addition to measures to control how judges manage their dockets, the Trump administration also sought to deport asylum seekers more frequently by hiring immigration judges and BIA members who were more likely to rule against asylum seekers. As early as 2007, research had shown that, on average, for every year that an immigration judge had served in a law enforcement job before becoming a prosecutor, the asylum grant rate for that individual, once on the bench, went down.[66] The Trump administration drew heavily on people with experience at DHS or the Department of Justice to fill the ranks of the immigration judges. Of the twenty-three immigration judges that Attorney General Sessions appointed in August 2018, "more than half previously worked with the Department of Homeland Security, and of those remaining, most came from a law enforcement background."[67] The next month, he appointed forty-six more judges, of whom nineteen had previously worked for ICE, and ten had worked as a federal or state prosecutor.[68]

Even more dramatically, the administration stacked the BIA with several people who, as immigration judges, had almost always ruled against asylum seekers. To do this, it first changed the structure of the BIA and the procedure for selecting and appointing its members. First, it expanded its size from seventeen to twenty-one members.[69] In the summer of 2019, there were six vacancies on the enlarged BIA. James McHenry, who had been appointed by Attorney General Sessions to be the executive director of the Executive Office for Immigration Review, considered only sitting immigration judges for the positions. This was a change from prior appointments, which had included candidates from the private sector, academia, or nonprofit organizations. Sessions then picked six immigration judges with asylum denial rates higher than 80 percent—three of whom had denial rates of 98, 96, and 92 percent—compared with a national average of 57 percent.[70] Two of the judges had the third- and fourth-highest rates, nationally, of cases being remanded by the BIA before their appointment to the BIA.[71] Furthermore, McHenry appointed these judges to permanent positions, eliminating the usual two-year probationary period. Paul W. Schmidt, a former BIA chair, commented that "the administration has weaponized the process"[72] and that the administration's goal was to build a "deportation railway."[73]

Decertifying the Immigration Judges' Union

Perhaps because it was unhappy with critiques of its procedures by officials of the immigration judges union, the National Association of Immigration Judges (NAIJ), the Trump administration took steps to decertify the union as the bargaining representative for the judges. To that end, it filed a petition with the Federal Labor Relations Authority, arguing that the judges were all management officials and therefore not entitled to be represented by a union. "It's absurd that anyone would consider us managers," Judge Tabaddor said. "We don't even have the authority to order pencils."[74]

The Federal Labor Relations Authority (FLRA) had rejected a similar claim by the Clinton administration in 2000. Its hearing officer insisted that before it considered the merits of the case, the Department of Justice would need to show that the judges' duties had changed since then. McHenry, Justice's main witness, conceded that the duties had not substantially changed but claimed that the "legal significance of those duties" had increased.[75] On July 31, 2020, the FLRA's hearing officer ruled in favor of the union.

The Trump administration then appealed to the full FLRA, which reversed the hearing officer in a 2–1 decision, decertifying the NAIJ as a union. It concluded that immigration judges are management officials because their decisions "influence the policy of the Agency [Executive Office for Immigration Review, EOIR]."[76] The stinging dissenting opinion characterized the majority's reasoning as "the antithesis of reasoned decision making" and concluded that "the majority's sole objective is to divest the IJs [immigration judges] of their statutory rights."[77] The NAIJ filed a motion for reconsideration and indicated that it would appeal to the federal courts.[78]

On July 1, 2020, the NAIJ sued the director of EOIR and the attorney general to challenge the administration's new policy, issued January 17, prohibiting immigration judges from speaking about immigration law and policy, including EOIR programs and policies, even in their personal capacity.[79] The NAIJ has appealed the denial of its motion for a preliminary injunction.[80]

Denying Legal Information to Detained Asylum Applicants

In 2003, the Bush administration began funding its Legal Orientation Program, the purpose of which was to "facilitate legal assistance from nonprofit organizations [such as the American Bar Association] for immigrant detainees in removal proceedings."[81] Across the country, nonprofit organizations provided hour-long "know-your-rights" presentations to detained migrants so that those who might qualify for asylum or other relief could know that they had a right to apply for protection. The presentations also helped those who had no chance of qualifying to understand that deportation was inevitable and that they could reduce their time in detention by consenting to an order of removal. Some of the nonprofit organizations also helped connect migrants who had strong asylum claims to lawyers who would advocate for them without charging a fee.[82]

In April 2018, the Trump administration announced that it was suspending the Legal Orientation Program's grants.[83] This announcement flew in the face of an analysis by EOIR itself that the program had saved the government almost $18 million between 2009 and 2011 by reducing the amount of time that immigrants spent in detention.[84] Faced with pressure from members of the Senate appropriations subcommittee that decides how much funding to provide to the Department of Justice, the administration temporarily restored the funding.[85]

Inaccurate Statistics and Country Conditions Information

Beginning in late 2019, EOIR made it virtually impossible for the public to assess the effects on asylum grant rates of the many procedural and substantive changes made by the Trump administration. Until then, it provided monthly statistical data on immigration court decisions to the Transactional Records Access Clearinghouse (TRAC) at Syracuse University. But TRAC noticed that thousands of applications for relief (e.g., asylum applications) went missing from the data beginning in October 2019. In April 2020, 68,282 applications that were present in the previous month's data release had disappeared from the data, more than the total number of asylum applications that the immigration courts received in all of 2015. Accordingly, TRAC warned that "any statistics EOIR has recently published" may be "suspect" and that "little faith can be placed in the factual accuracy of reports published by EOIR based on its data."[86]

In a parallel display of inaccuracy, the Trump administration's State Department issued annual human rights country conditions reports that severely downplayed human rights violations in certain countries. Asylum officers and immigration judges rely heavily on those reports to determine whether asylum seekers' testimony is consistent with known facts about the countries from which they have fled. These inaccurate reports misled adjudicators in a variety of ways. Perhaps unsurprisingly, the State Department downplayed rights violations in Honduras.[87] In addition, the State Department reports on violations of women's rights, civil and political rights, and issues relating to LGTBQ+ persons in Eritrea, Iran, Iraq, Pakistan, and Sudan were reportedly inconsistent with the degree of violence committed against victims of persecution in those countries.[88]

The administration also tried to change reporting by U.S. intelligence agencies on human rights conditions in Central America. The DHS Office of Inspector General found that, in December 2019, Kenneth Cuccinelli, then holding the title of senior official performing the duties of the director of USCIS, attempted to alter information in intelligence reports used by asylum officers to understand country conditions in El Salvador, Guatemala, and Honduras. Though these reports were consistent with previous reports detailing substantial violence and corruption in these countries, Cuccinelli apparently "accused unknown 'deep state intelligence analysts' of compiling the intelligence information to undermine President Donald J. Trump's policy objectives with respect to asylum."[89] In other words, Cuccinelli attempted to water down reports that asylum seekers faced serious harms in these countries so that asylum officers could deny their claims to protection, and he became angry when analysts insisted on presenting truthful and accurate reports.

It comes as no surprise, therefore, that the rate at which immigration courts denied asylum increased dramatically during the Trump administration. The denial rate was 55 percent during the last year of the Obama administration, but it reached a record high of 72 percent in fiscal year 2020.[90]

4

THE BORDER SHUTDOWN EXECUTED BY THE TRUMP ADMINISTRATION

The Refugee Act of 1980 established access to asylum for all those who arrive at U.S. borders. This law makes it clear that no matter how an asylum seeker arrives, he or she is entitled to ask for asylum.[1] For well more than three decades, the executive branch ensured that asylum seekers could seek protection in the United States whether they arrived at an air or land port of entry with or without a visa or crossed the land border without permission. That changed under Donald Trump.

At the center of his campaign for the presidency of the United States, Trump promised to build a wall across the southern border. He systematically built a virtual "wall" out of regulations, policies, and practices, and he ended the opportunities created by the Refugee Act of 1980 for asylum seekers to find a safe haven in the United States when they arrive at the southern border. As a National Security Council official aptly described, the Trump administration's "mantra has persistently been presenting aliens with multiple unsolvable dilemmas to impact their calculus for choosing to make the arduous journey to begin with."[2]

Until June 2020, his administration created policy after policy in an extraordinary attack on asylum that resulted in successfully excluding refugees at the Mexican border. The analysis in this chapter discusses the restrictions that the Trump administration imposed at the southern border of the United States.

Screening for Credible Fear

In contrast to the previous Democratic and Republican administrations, the Trump administration saw in the expedited removal procedure an opportunity to quickly reject many asylum applicants. Speedy denials at the initial screening stage would prevent asylum seekers from having the opportunity to engage lawyers or to present evidence to immigration judges, some of whom would undoubtedly be sympathetic to the plight of those who claimed fear of persecution.[3]

When the administration took office, the asylum officers who conducted the credible fear interviews for asylum applicants were honoring the law, applying a "low screening standard" to their interviewees.[4] As Congress intended, the Department of Homeland Security (DHS) used these interviews to weed out only the very weakest cases, thereby giving those who might be at risk of persecution a chance to present their claims in court. As a result, DHS was finding credible fear on the part of the vast majority of asylum applicants in the expedited removal process, thereby providing them with access to immigration court hearings. In fiscal year 2016, asylum officers found that 80 percent of applicants had a credible fear of persecution.[5] Even in the early years of the Trump administration, the rate of positive determinations remained high: 77 percent in fiscal year 2018.[6]

The guidance for officers who perform the screenings is contained in a "lesson plan" that the asylum office headquarters uses to train its officers. The Trump administration sought to decrease the number of asylum applicants determined to have a credible fear by changing the instructions in the lesson plan.[7] Through amendments to the plan in 2017 and particularly in April 2019, it made four important changes.[8]

First, before the Trump administration, the lesson plans stated that the "applicant must establish that there is a significant possibility that the assertions underlying his or her claim could be found credible" by an immigration judge. The Trump administration eliminated this language in favor of providing that "an asylum officer should assess the credibility of the assertions underlying [the claim], considering the totality of the circumstances, including other statements made by the applicant, evidence of country conditions, State Department reports, and all other relevant facts and evidence."[9] In other words, rather than determining whether it was possible that the claim would be credible, the officers were assessing credibility in an expedited process that was not designed to accurately examine such complex factual questions.

Second, the administration suggested that corroboration was relevant even at the screening stage. Most applicants fleeing from persecution do not bring evidence with them, so they cannot present such corroboration during credible fear interviews that generally take place within days after they enter the United States. The administration's 2019 version of the lesson plan eliminated prior text stating that "oftentimes, in the credible fear context of expedited removal and detention, an applicant will not be able to provide additional evidence corroborating his or her otherwise credible testimony. An applicant may establish a credible fear with testimony alone if that testimony is detailed, consistent, and plausible."[10]

The Trump administration's new guidance provided, instead, that "under the [REAL ID Act], the asylum officer is also entitled to determine that the applicant must provide evidence that corroborates the applicant's testimony, even where the officer might otherwise find the testimony credible. In cases in which the asylum officer determines that the applicant must provide such evidence, the asylum officer must provide the applicant notice and the opportunity to submit evidence, and the applicant *must* provide the evidence unless the applicant cannot reasonably obtain the evidence" (emphasis in the original).[11]

The third change concerned situations in which federal courts of appeals disagreed about interpretations of the law. One federal circuit's interpretation might favor the applicant's claim, while another's might make it less likely that the applicant would be granted asylum. At credible fear screenings, it is impossible to know where in the United States applicants will be living by the time of their immigration court hearings (and consequently which federal circuit's law would apply). Prior lesson plans therefore provided that the law to be applied, in absence of policy guidance from U.S. Citizenship and Immigration Services (USCIS), was the law of the circuit that was most favorable to the applicant. The Trump administration's guidance provided, in a footnote, that the law to be applied was that of the circuit where the applicant was located at the time of the screening interview.[12] Because the longest southern border is in Texas, this meant that in many cases, the legal standards applied to most interviews would be those of the Fifth Circuit, which tended to be much less favorable to the asylum seeker than the legal standards of the other federal circuits.

Fourth, the administration's new guidance required asylum officers conducting credible fear interviews to reject candidates based on several legal determinations that, under the law, should have instead been made by immigration judges in full asylum hearings. For example, the officers were instructed that "if the evidence does not establish . . . reasons why internal relocation is not possible, a negative credible fear determination is appropriate."

In October 2020, a federal district court vacated the Trump administration's changes in the credible fear screening process. It held that DHS had "imported the standards and burdens that apply only during full removal proceedings into the expedited removal screening process [and made] pronouncements about the law that clash" with the expedited removal standards in the statute itself. For example, the court cited the corroboration requirement in the new standards, and their insistence that the candidate for a credible fear determination prove that internal relocation was not possible. According to the court, the new guidance "contradicts the unambiguous text" of the asylum law and requires the court to void the administration's guidance. The Trump administration promptly appealed.[13]

A second way in which the Trump administration apparently sought to affect the credible fear grant rate was by changing the personnel conducting the screenings. Consistent with the intent of Congress,[14] the interviews had always been conducted by USCIS asylum officers, who receive six weeks of basic training, three weeks of specific training on credible fear, and four hours of informal training per week.[15]

In June 2019, the administration began assigning Border Patrol officers to conduct the interviews.[16] These officers received some training on their new tasks but not nearly as much training as asylum officers. They reportedly also lack an appropriate cultural mind-set for the work. As Michael Knowles, a special representative for the federal asylum officers' union, explained, many asylum officers "are concerned about the use of law enforcement personnel for crucial interviews with people seeking refuge."[17] Another DHS official was more direct, stating that "Border Patrol can't get out of the law enforcement mentality. They think they are supposed to 'break' asylum seekers."[18] Asylum officers are trained to ask many questions to ensure that they have comprehensively assessed the viability of any legal claim.[19] The ability of Border Patrol officers to question asylum seekers in a neutral and nonadversarial manner about inconsistencies with statements that they previously made to the Border Patrol agents who originally apprehended them is questionable at best given their relative lack of training in this skill and their cultural mind-set.[20]

It is perhaps not surprising that in the year June 2019 to

June 2020, Border Patrol agents had a 35 percent grant rate for credible fear interviews while asylum officers had a 55 percent grant rate.[21] As one asylum officer noted, "The administration has been successful in subverting the law and the will of Congress in setting standards."[22] In August 2020, a federal court preliminarily enjoined Border Patrol officers from conducting credible fear interviews because this practice violated the Refugee Act as amended.[23] The decision is subject to appeal.[24]

Tearing Families Apart

Perhaps the most shocking of Trump's immigration policies, and the only one that generated a massive public outcry, was his administration's program that tore thousands of children from their parents. Many of the families that were split apart were applicants for asylum.[25] In 2018 and 2019, many Central American asylum seekers consisted of what CBP called "family units," a dehumanizing term describing mostly mothers who crossed the border, either at ports of entry or irregularly, along with their children, some of whom were infants or toddlers.

Despite very high rates of appearance in court by asylum-seeking families, Trump ended an Obama-era policy known as the Family Case Management Program in June 2017. The program released families from prison with social work support to help them apply for housing, welfare, and school and to show up to hearings.[26] Participants in this program had a 99 percent appearance rate in court,[27] and the program cost the federal government $38 per day as opposed to $319 per day to keep a family in prison.[28] At about the same time, the administration then began to arrest undocumented parents who came to pick up their children who had been temporarily in the custody of the Office of Refugee Resettlement after crossing the border alone.[29] In some cases, the administration then threatened the parents with prosecution under antismuggling laws for sending money to help their children cross the border. In other cases, the administration detained the parents for deportation.[30]

Arresting some parents of unaccompanied minors was merely a lead-up to the horrors of family separation. Even without a policy in place, in March 2017, government statistics show an increase of nearly 900 percent in family separations.[31] The following month, in a stark about-face from prior policy, Attorney General Jeff Sessions directed federal prosecutors to prioritize the prosecution of asylum seekers, particularly families.[32] CBP began its secretive Family Separation Pilot Program in July 2017 in El Paso, separating at least 280 families over five months.[33] During this pilot, border agents in the field informed CBP headquarters that the agency's records systems prevented officials from keeping track of separated children and their parents, but headquarters staff failed to fix the problem.[34]

A planning document written in December 2017, which was shared among Department of Justice (DOJ) and DHS officials, described a plan to prosecute parents for illegal entry into the United States and then quite publicly to put their children in Department of Health and Human Services (HHS) custody as unaccompanied minors, with the belief that widespread media coverage of removing children from their mothers would have a deterrent effect.[35] The American Civil Liberties Union (ACLU) was alerted to the family separation policy shortly after the El Paso pilot program ended, filing a case in February 2018 that challenged the separation of one mother and daughter who eventually represented the entire class of separated families.[36]

In April 2018, Sessions issued the "Zero Tolerance" memo that required federal prosecutors to criminally prosecute all adults who crossed the southwest border without inspection.[37] Sessions said that "we need to take away children," and Deputy Attorney General Rod Rosenstein told U.S. attorneys in border states that it did not matter how young the children were.[38] Despite the finding by a federal judge that deterring migrants was an impermissible justification for jailing migrants who were in the United States, the Trump administration made its deterrent aims crystal clear.[39] In an interview with NPR in May 2018, then–DHS secretary John Kelly said, "a big name of the game is deterrence. . . . It could be a tough deterrent—would be a tough deterrent." Evincing little interest in the welfare of the children, he added, "The children will be taken care of—put into foster care or whatever."[40]

The separations of thousands of families followed, and publicity about it resulted in a national and international uproar. Videos of very young, crying children being torn away from a mother or father by Border Patrol agents shocked the consciences of many, including Trump supporters.[41] Protests across the political spectrum were voiced by, among many others, Ivanka Trump, thirteen Republican senators, the American Catholic bishops, and the pope. Trump backed down, claiming to end the family separation policy, but he did not agree to reunite the families whose members had been separated. Reunification was ordered in June, however, by the federal judge in the case filed by the ACLU.[42]

Nobody knows the exact number of children separated from their families because of the government's shocking negligence; its failure to keep track of separated children means that we know that the government separated at least 2,800 children from their parents,[43] but other sources report the number to be over 5,000.[44] A total of 666 families still remained separated as of November 2020.[45] A federal judge and federal watchdogs for DOJ, DHS, and HHS as well as the Government Accountability Office found that the administration had developed no plan to reunify these separated families.[46] Indeed, DHS officials at the highest level failed to take even the most rudimentary steps to keep track of separated children and their parents.[47]

To eliminate any roadblocks to its efforts to detain children, the Trump administration attempted to modify and supersede the *Flores* settlement agreement, which the government had signed in 1997. That settlement barred holding children in jail-like detention facilities and mandated that they could be incarcerated only in nonsecure *state-licensed* child protection facilities. In 2015, federal Judge Dolly Gee, who oversees the *Flores* settlement, had held that the agreement applied to both children who entered with an adult and also to unaccompanied children. She also authorized jailing the children for up to twenty days for processing,[48] and the U.S. Court of Appeals for the Ninth Circuit had affirmed that holding.[49]

In June 2018, after Trump allegedly ended the family separation policy, the attorney general asked Judge Gee to grant limited emergency relief to extend the period of detention for minors beyond twenty days and to enable the administration to hold minors in unlicensed facilities.[50] Less than a month later, Judge Gee rejected the government's arguments.[51] In response to Judge Gee's ruling, the Trump administration tried to end the *Flores* agreement by issuing regulations covering the detention of children. The proposed regulations explicitly allowed the government to jail children who had entered with family members in a facility licensed by Immigration and Customs Enforcement (ICE) rather than by the state, which would have enabled the government to keep the parents and their children together, and to jail them for years, until immigration courts could make final decisions on their asylum applications.[52]

While the new regulation was in its notice and comment period, Attorney General Barr attempted to shore up family detention. In April 2019, he referred to himself *Matter of M-S-*, which he used to hold that ICE could not release asylum applicants who have passed a credible fear interview even if they were able to pay bond.[53] The decision was enjoined by the Ninth Circuit,[54] but in 2021, the Supreme Court reversed the injunction and required the Ninth Circuit to reconsider it in the light of the high court's recent holding that migrants in the expedited removal process may not seek a writ of habeas corpus to obtain court review of their detention.[55] Meanwhile, even as representation for bond hearings in immigration courts has increased, the rate at which immigration judges have granted bond to immigrants has dropped since 2018.[56]

In 2019, when the Trump administration promulgated the final rule to abrogate the *Flores* agreement,[57] the attorneys general of more than twenty states sought an injunction against the rule.[58] Judge Gee rejected the regulation, issuing a permanent injunction against it. She found the regulation "inconsistent with one of the primary goals of the *Flores* agreement, which is to instate a general policy favoring release and expeditiously place minors in the least restrictive setting appropriate to the minor's age and special needs." In December 2020, the U.S. Court of Appeals affirmed her ruling, holding that the administration's plan to have ICE license family detention facilities in states that do not do so "greatly expands DHS's ability to detain minors with their accompanying adults" and that what the *Flores* agreement contemplated was "an open setting, such as a foster or group home, and not a detention facility." [59]

Though the Trump administration has repeatedly been enjoined in its efforts to tear apart families and lock up children, it has been successful in cabining the protections against jailing that had been available to some children. Under the Obama administration, a child who filed for asylum before the age of eighteen would be held in the custody of the Office of Refugee Resettlement (ORR) rather than in jail and would have the asylum application adjudicated as an initial matter by an asylum officer rather than an immigration judge. But the Board of Immigration Appeals decided that the regulations that govern protections for children do not apply once a child turns eighteen.[60] As a result, on their eighteenth birthday, children in ORR custody were transferred to the much harsher conditions of ICE detention centers. There they would face adversarial immigration court hearings (rather than nonadversarial asylum officer interviews).[61] Two years later, however, a federal judge held that the government was violating the law by automatically transferring these individuals to detention in an ICE facility for adults, and should instead consider the less restrictive alternatives of placing them with sponsoring relatives, releasing them on bond, or releasing them with ankle bracelets while they waited for their hearings.[62]

Whether the harshness of detention actually deters women and children from seeking asylum in the United States, the Trump administration relied on this rationale to separate and jail countless families seeking protection in the United States. Most recently, during the COVID-19 pandemic, DHS has reinstated a plan called "binary choice," forcing parents in family jails to make "the torturous 'choice' of keeping their children indefinitely detained in conditions that one federal court has described as 'hotbeds for contagion' or being separated from them."[63] The Trump administration sought an order from Judge Gee to permit binary choice agreements under the *Flores* agreement.[64]

Pushbacks and Metering

After Trump's election, at some ports of entry Customs and Border Protection officers informally pushed back asylum seekers into Mexico by threatening them or misinforming them about their rights.[65] CBP officers reportedly told asylum seekers that "Trump says we don't have to let you in" and "the United States is not giving asylum anymore." Officers also instructed applicants without any basis that they did not qualify for asylum and that they would go to prison for years, pressured them to recant statements that they feared being

returned to their home country, produced statements that
falsely indicated no such fear, or threatened to take their children away.[66] In some circumstances, CBP officers began processing asylum seekers at ports of entry but then coerced them
into signing forms waiving their asylum claims.[67] These illegal
practices became more widespread after President Trump was
inaugurated.[68] The DHS inspector general found that in 2018,
CBP stopped processing almost all asylum seekers at seven
ports of entry, and "although asylum seekers legally must be
processed once physically within the United States," officials
had turned away those who had already entered the United
States at four ports of entry.[69]

The Trump administration also adopted a policy of "metering," in which CBP officers refused to process asylum seekers who presented themselves at ports of entry on the United
States–Mexico border. CBP officers stood on the bridges to
the United States, preventing the asylum seekers from reaching the U.S. border a few yards away where they could access
Refugee Act protections. They put the refugees on wait-lists
and instructed them to come back weeks or months later.[70]
Metering became official CBP policy for all southern border
ports in April 2018, although no formal guidance on the policy has been released to the public.[71]

The administration justified metering by claiming that it
prevented overcrowding at processing centers, but the DHS
Office of Inspector General found that asylum seekers were
turned back, at least at the Tecate Port of Entry, regardless of
capacity.[72] In *Al Otro Lado v. Wolf*, a class action challenge to
the metering practice, the plaintiffs acknowledged that the
government had a legitimate interest in preventing overcrowding at the centers but claimed that the purported justification
was pretextual and that the real purpose of metering was to
deter asylum seekers. A federal district court denied DHS's
motion to dismiss the case[73] and granted class action status

to the case.[74] In October 2020, that court ordered DHS and EOIR to reopen or reconsider past decisions denying asylum to those who had been metered and were marooned in Mexico when the Second Asylum Ban, discussed below, took effect.[75]

Because DHS has not provided data to the public, the total number of asylum seekers metered even since the April 2018 inception of metering as an official policy cannot be determined accurately. Research centers at the University of Texas and the University of California, San Diego, have reported quarterly snapshots showing that wait-lists reached as high as 26,000 in August 2019.[76] By February 2020, at least 15,000 asylum seekers were still waiting in eleven Mexican border cities to enter the United States after having been subjected to metering.[77] In March 2020, many wait-lists closed to new asylum seekers when CBP began removing those seeking safety through a new COVID-19 expulsion policy (discussed below).[78] More than 14,500 asylum seekers were still on wait-lists as of late May 2020.[79] Some of those metered by DHS were assaulted and raped while waiting their turn for processing.[80]

Trump's First Asylum Ban

Despite increased metering, asylum seekers continued to arrive at the southern border of the United States in 2018, especially from the Northern Triangle countries.[81] DHS responded with increasingly harsh policies to prevent these forced migrants from accessing asylum. Litigators challenged each policy.

The first new policy was a ban on asylum for the majority of Central American asylum applicants—those who entered the United States at places other than ports of entry. When Congress created the expedited removal screening system in 1996, it recognized that many refugees fled to the United States in any way possible and that they did not always enter through an official port of entry. Congress explicitly provided that a migrant could seek asylum even if they entered the United States by crossing the Rio Grande in an irregular manner: "Any alien who is physically present in the United States or *who arrives in the United States (whether or not at a designated port of arrival and including an alien who is brought to the United States after having been interdicted in international or United States waters), irrespective of such alien's status, may apply for asylum.*"[82]

Nonetheless, in November 2018, DOJ and DHS issued a rule that made asylum seekers who crossed the border outside of legal entry stations along the southern border "ineligible for asylum" if subject to a presidential proclamation suspending or limiting their entry on this border.[83] President Trump simultaneously issued a proclamation stating that those who enter without inspection—that is, other than at an official port of entry—would be "ineligible to be granted asylum."[84]

Ten days later, the U.S. District Court for the Northern District of California issued a temporary restraining order blocking implementation of this rule.[85] On December 7, 2018, the Ninth Circuit declined to stay the order;[86] and on December 19, 2018, the Northern District of California followed up with a preliminary nationwide injunction.[87] The Supreme Court also declined to stay the injunction,[88] and the Ninth Circuit eventually affirmed the nationwide injunction.[89]

Writing for the majority of the Ninth Circuit panel in denying the government's emergency motion for a stay pending appeal, Judge Jay Bybee framed the administration's attempt to avoid the congressional asylum statute, Section 1158, in this way: "Just as we may not, as we are often reminded, 'legislate from the bench,' neither may the Executive legislate from the Oval Office."[90] Undaunted, the Trump administration quickly put into place other rules and policies to deter asylum seekers and restrict their access to asylum.

Migrant Protection Protocols (Remain in Mexico)

In December 2018, just as the administration was losing its bar on asylum for migrants who entered the United States irregularly, the Trump administration adopted its Migrant Protection Protocols (MPP), otherwise known as the "Remain in Mexico" plan. This DHS-operated program requires that asylum seekers arriving on the United States–Mexico border return to Mexican border towns to wait until the completion of their immigration court proceedings.[91] No previous administration, Republican or Democratic, has ever implemented a policy returning asylum seekers to Mexico to await their hearings or believed that Congress had authorized such a policy.[92] By April 2020, more than 65,000 asylum seekers, including 16,000 children and 500 infants, had been removed to Mexico through MPP.[93] Hundreds of them were especially vulnerable, including "children with cancer, autism, cerebral palsy, and brain seizures, adults with limited mental capacity, seizure disorders, and at least two deaf, nonverbal individuals, many pregnant women and LGBTQ+ persons, as well as dozens of Mexican nationals and at least one unaccompanied child who are not even eligible for MPP."[94] Many were families with children.[95]

Those forced to wait in Mexico have suffered serious violence there, including rape, kidnapping,[96] and robbery by members of drug cartels, traffickers, and other criminals operating in border cities: "Organized crime lookouts, called *halcones* (hawks), 'are everywhere near the port of entry,' and some MPP returnees have been kidnapped on the street just outside the reception area. Kidnappers demand ransom from relatives in the United States; 'it usually starts at US$10,000, then gets negotiated down to $3,000 to $5,000.'"[97] DHS even returns asylum seekers who seek entry along the border from Brownsville to Laredo, Texas, to the Mexican state of

Tamaulipas. The State Department has assigned Tamaulipas the highest level "DO NOT TRAVEL" advisory—the same warning it has designated for Afghanistan, Syria, and Yemen.[98] By November 2019, Human Rights First documented more than 1,000 cases of rape, kidnapping, assault, extortion, and other crimes against migrants forced to remain in Mexico.[99]

Shelter space in Mexico was limited. One-third of those returned to Tijuana and Mexicali suffered periods of homelessness. Such camps as existed could not meet children's medical needs. In one Matamoros camp, children suffered from "malnutrition, severe flu, appendicitis, fistula, sepsis, and other life-threatening conditions." Children expressed fears of human traffickers targeting the camp, "including a young girl who said an unknown man approached her, held his hand up to indicate her height, and said that she was about the 'right size.'"[100]

Metering wait times grew in the months after MPP was implemented.[101] Many were ordered deported in absentia because they were unable to attend their court hearings. Some had been kidnapped, others did not receive notice of their hearing date, many found it too unsafe to wait in Mexico for long periods of time, and still others could not make the perilous journey to the assigned border crossing.

The MPP program forced tens of thousands of migrants to wait in Mexico for their immigration court hearings, but it did not extinguish their right to a hearing. This presented the Executive Office for Immigration Review with a logistical problem: How would it provide hearings for thousands of people who were living in makeshift shelters in another country? How would it even find them to notify them about where and when their hearings would take place? How would it get them to the courtrooms?

The Trump administration's solution to this problem of its own making was yet another short circuit of due process. When DHS forced migrants over the border into Mexico, it told them to keep the government informed of their addresses there, but many had to move around frequently, and others lived on the street. This made it impossible for DHS to serve them with notices stating where and when to appear to be escorted back across the border for hearings. When DHS did not know where the migrants were, it sent hearing notices to Facebook or to a shelter of which the migrants had never heard.[102] These notices often could not be delivered, resulting in many migrants missing their hearings[103] and being deported in absentia.[104]

Those who did appear were required to arrive at a designated border crossing several hours before proceedings began at 8:30 a.m. Then many were taken to tents along the U.S.-Mexican border that the Trump administration designated as "courts." There were no judges in these tent courts,[105] only TV monitors on which the migrant could see a judge who might be hundreds of miles away in a courtroom with the opposing ICE lawyer and an interpreter. Restrooms nearby consisted of porta-potties.[106]

Very few migrants in the MPP system had legal representation, because U.S. lawyers could not easily communicate with them in Mexico, especially privately, while they waited to be called for hearings, and the migrants were not allowed into the United States to prepare their cases with lawyers.[107] Some immigration judges sympathized with the migrants' needs for additional time to try to find a lawyer. In those cases, asylum seekers had to take many dangerous round trips over several months between the tent court and whatever housing they could find in Mexico.[108]

The Trump administration hoped that the MPP would deliver a deterrent message and discourage new arrivals of asylum seekers at the southern border. But as figure 4.1 shows, such arrivals actually increased significantly in February 2019, shortly after DHS implemented MPP, and the number of new

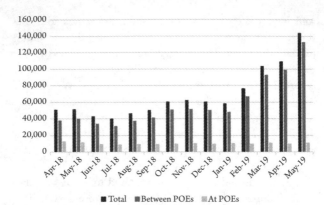

Figure 4.1 Arrivals at the U.S. Southern Border, April 2018–May 2019

Sources: U.S. Customs and Border Protection, Southwest Border Migration FY2018, https://www.cbp.gov/newsroom/stats/sw-border-migration/fy-2018; Southwest Border Migration FY2019, https://www.cbp.gov/news room/stats/sw-border-migration/fy-2019.

Note: POE = port of entry.

arrivals reached a new thirteen-year record high level in May 2019.[109]

In response, Trump threatened Mexico with tariffs via Twitter: "On June 10th, the United States will impose a 5% Tariff on all goods coming into our Country from Mexico, until such time as illegal migrants coming through Mexico, and into our Country, STOP. The Tariff will gradually increase until the Illegal Immigration problem is remedied."[110]

Mexico then quickly committed to deploying its National Guard throughout the country, "giving priority to its southern border." It also committed to accepting larger numbers of MPP returnees.[111] Mexico's dramatic increase in enforcement at its southern border, tripling year-over-year apprehensions in

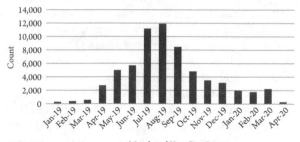

Figure 4.2 Asylum Seekers Forced to Remain in Mexico (MPP)

Source: TRAC Immigration, Details on MPP (Remain in Mexico) Deportation Proceedings, https://trac.syr.edu/phptools/immigration/mpp/.

June 2019, pushed asylum seekers to more dangerous routes of transit through the country.[112] Mexico also accepted many more MPP returnees, a decision that led to the resignation of the head of the Mexican Instituto Nacional de Migración, who consistently and clearly stated that Mexico did not have the capacity to receive and protect these asylum seekers.[113]

As the MPP monthly bar chart given in figure 4.2 shows, the Mexico–United States cooperation on MPP stepped up considerably immediately after the tariff threat. The number of asylum seekers forced to wait in Mexico in April and May—about 2,600 and 5,100—jumped to some 11,600 and 12,400 in July and August.

CBP placed more than 69,000 asylum seekers into MPP. Of those for whom the immigration courts purportedly scheduled at least one hearing, more than half were ordered deported in absentia. Almost 27,000 cases were still pending as of November 2020.[114] Immigration judges only granted relief to some 600, or about 1.5 percent of those who received decisions.[115] Only 7 percent of asylum seekers in MPP were able to locate attorneys to represent them in their proceedings.[116] In a number of cases, DHS flagrantly disregarded immigration judges' grants of asylum and returned refugees to Mexico.[117] If the administration's goal was to make it nearly impossible for the people consigned to the MPP program to win relief, the program was extraordinarily successful.

As discussed in chapter 2, the legality of MPP depends on an obscure provision of the immigration law, added in 1996, that allows the executive branch under certain circumstances to return a noncitizen requesting admission to a contiguous territory while awaiting a decision.[118] The provision arguably does not apply to asylum applicants who could be subjected to expedited removal. Specifically, the provision applies only to "an alien described in subparagraph (A)" of Section 1225(b)(2), which exempts from its coverage migrants who arrive without proper documents and therefore are subject to expedited removal.[119] The administration took the view that the provision could be applied if it used its discretion to place a person subject to expedited removal into "regular" removal proceedings. It could then make such a person wait in Mexico until a regular removal hearing could be arranged.

In a challenge brought by immigration advocacy organizations, a federal district court judge issued a preliminary injunction against MPP.[120] A Ninth Circuit panel granted the government's motion for an emergency stay,[121] and it eventually affirmed the district court's grant of the preliminary injunction, confirming that the provision does not apply to asylum seekers.[122] In an extraordinary step, the union representing asylum officers filed an amicus brief in that case, explaining that MPP violates the United States' international legal commitments and is simply unnecessary as our immigration system is agile enough to address large flows of asylum seekers and adjudicate claims efficiently.[123] The Supreme Court, however, stayed the preliminary injunction until it could consider whether to decide the matter itself, a stay that has allowed the government to continue implementing MPP.[124] In October 2020, the Supreme Court decided to hear the case, and unless the Biden administration withdraws the appeal, the Court will issue a decision in the spring of 2021.[125] With tens of thousands of asylum seekers waiting in Mexico under MPP for their immigration hearings, immigration advocacy organizations brought a new challenge later that month seeking to require DHS to allow these asylum seekers into the United States to pursue their court cases.[126]

Trump's Second Asylum Ban

Having been enjoined from implementing the first ban in November 2018, and frustrated by the increasing arrivals at the southern border, the Trump administration doubled down by issuing a second asylum ban in the form of an interim final rule, effective in mid-July 2019. This rule eliminates eligibility for asylum for almost everyone who seeks asylum at the southern border without having first applied for and been denied asylum in Mexico or another country through which they passed en route. Commonly called the Third Country Transit Bar (TCTB), this second ban is even more stringent than the first, for it applies not only to people who cross the border without permission but also to those who present themselves at a port of entry to request asylum. Furthermore, this ban applies alike to unaccompanied children, families, and single adults, and not only to Latin Americans but also to Africans and others who initially fled to South America before arriving at the U.S. border.[127]

From the perspective of the Trump administration, one important design feature of this ban is that it makes all Central Americans, among others, ineligible for asylum. This enables the government to place all these asylum seekers into the expedited removal process and then, because these individuals would have no possibility of winning asylum, summarily determine that they fail the credible fear test. The government still needs to interview them to determine whether they have a "reasonable fear" of persecution. In other words, the asylum seeker must show that there is a "reasonable" chance of proving to an immigration judge that persecution in the home country is more likely than not—as opposed to the credible fear test, in which an applicant only has to show a significant possibility of proving a "well-founded fear" of persecution.[128] If the executive finds that an asylum applicant is barred from asylum and fails the "reasonable fear" test, it can remove that asylum seeker immediately. Even applicants who meet this standard and then win before an immigration judge are eligible only for withholding of removal. In contrast to those granted asylum, they have no path to permanent residence and citizenship and cannot rely on their legal status to protect their close family members.

The Trump administration has used the transit ban to deny asylum to hundreds of refugees, according to a report by Human Rights First.[129] Even after determining that applicants established that they risked being persecuted or tortured if returned to their home country, immigration judges denied them asylum based on the TCTB. These applicants included a "Cameroonian man tortured by the military, an LGBTQ+ woman from Honduras who was beaten, repeatedly raped, and kidnapped by gangs because of her sexual orientation, a Cuban political activist detained, beaten, and threatened with death for supporting the Damas de Blanco (Ladies in White), a Cuban opposition movement founded by female relatives of jailed dissidents, and a Venezuelan opposition supporter kidnapped and tortured by pro-government forces."[130] Immigration judges also denied asylum and other forms of protection to applicants such as a "Venezuelan opposition journalist and her one-year-old child and a Cuban asylum seeker who was beaten and subjected to forced labor due to his political activity."[131]

Pursuant to the 1980 Refugee Act, previous administrations have granted asylum to tens of thousands of refugees who entered the United States from Mexico and who passed through other countries en route to America. Congress never established a policy of requiring migrants to seek asylum en route to the United States. In fact, the asylum statute bars refugees who transit through other countries from asylum only if they "firmly resettled" in the transit country[132] or if the United States has a formal return agreement with a country where refugees are both safe from persecution and would have access to a full and fair procedure to seek asylum.[133] The regulations define "firm resettlement" as citizenship, permanent resident status, or the equivalent.[134] As further discussed below, the United States has only one safe third-country agreement, with Canada.[135]

The government's legal justification for the ban is based on a provision in the immigration law stating that in addition to the bars on asylum for those who were already firmly resettled in another country, or whose claims must be adjudicated in a safe country with which the United States has a formal agreement, the attorney general may "by regulation establish additional limitations and conditions, consistent with this section [that is 8 U.S.C. Sec. 1158, providing for asylum] under which an alien shall be ineligible for asylum."[136] The legal issue boils down to whether a ban on virtually all non-Mexicans arriving via Mexico is "consistent" with a statute that does not contain any other bans that sweep so broadly, but rather excludes much narrower categories of asylum applicants.

A federal court in California enjoined the TCTB,[137] but the Supreme Court stayed the injunction without writing an opinion,[138] just as it had with the injunction against MPP, thereby reinstating the rule nationwide. Justices Sotomayor and Ginsburg, dissenting, pointed out that

Section 1158 generally provides that any noncitizen "physically present in the United States or who arrives in

the United States . . . may apply for asylum." § 1158(a)
(1). And unlike the rule, the District Court explained, the
statute provides narrow, carefully calibrated exceptions
to asylum eligibility. As relevant here, Congress restricted
asylum based on the possibility that a person could safely
resettle in a third country. . . . The rule, by contrast, does
not consider whether refugees were safe or resettled in
Mexico—just whether they traveled through it. That
blunt approach, according to the District Court, rewrote
the statute. . . . A "mountain of evidence points one
way," the District Court observed, yet the Government
"went the other—with no explanation."[139]

On July 6, 2020, the Ninth Circuit affirmed the lower court's
preliminary injunction regarding the transit ban, holding that
the rule is unlawful under the Administrative Procedures Act.
The panel concluded that the rule is inconsistent with the asylum statute because it does virtually nothing to ensure that a
third country is a safe option.[140]

On June 30, 2020, in a separate case, a federal court in the
District of Columbia vacated the interim TCTB rule, holding
that the Trump administration had violated the Administrative Procedures Act.[141] However, in its final days, the Trump
administration replaced the interim final rule with a final rule
to the same effect. Because the final rule had been subjected to
the required notice and comment procedures, this had the effect of circumventing the federal court's decision. The administration made the final rule effective on January 19, 2021, its
last day in office.[142] The final rule is subject to the objections
articulated by the Ninth Circuit in its affirmance of the district
court's injunction against the TCTB, because those objections
challenged the rule on the merits rather than the procedures
through which the rule was promulgated. As noted above, that
ruling was stayed by the Supreme Court.

Asylum Cooperative Agreements

The TCTB did not fulfill the administration's goal of ending asylum. For one thing, it exempted Mexicans because they had not transited through another country. For another, even though asylum seekers arriving through Mexico could summarily be denied credible fear, and therefore asylum, they could still possibly meet the "reasonable fear" standard. If these applicants could then establish in an immigration court their eligibility for withholding of removal or protection under the Convention Against Torture, they could remain in the United States.

So the administration took more steps to dismantle the asylum system. First, it stretched the section of the immigration law that authorized the executive branch to establish bilateral or multilateral agreements with "safe third" countries, where refugees would not be subject to persecution and where asylum seekers would have access to "a full and fair procedure for determining a claim to asylum or equivalent temporary protection."[143] Previous administrations had established only one such agreement, with Canada; that agreement was concluded after more than three years of detailed negotiations that included serious consideration of public comments.[144]

The Trump administration initially pursued what it wanted to call a safe third-country agreement with Mexico, hoping that threats of imposing tariffs on Mexican goods would bring such a result during the summer of 2019. But Mexico's government refused to sign such an agreement because it "would have compelled it indefinitely to take all non-Mexican asylum seekers who cross through its territory."[145]

After President Trump also threatened to impose tariffs on Central American exports,[146] the administration was able to sign three separate Asylum Cooperative Agreements (ACA) with each of the three Northern Triangle countries from which many asylum seekers were fleeing:[147] El Salvador, Guatemala,

and Honduras. These agreements were concluded after less
than two months of considerable economic pressure by the
Trump administration.[148] In November 2019, the Trump administration issued an interim final rule authorizing DHS to
implement all three agreements.[149] By the end of November
2020, only the Guatemala ACA had been implemented.[150]
That ACA enabled the administration to circumvent the Refugee Act and deport adult asylum applicants who were not
Guatemalan citizens to Guatemala without allowing them to
apply for asylum in the United States.[151]

In principle, the three agreements could enable DHS to
return nearly every Honduran or Salvadoran asylum seeker to
Guatemala, and every Guatemalan asylum seeker to Honduras
or El Salvador, even though the same gangs from which many
are fleeing have a powerful presence in each country. Moreover,
any refugee from any other country in the world could be sent
to any of those nations that lack any semblance of an asylum
process and in which they would likely be targeted by the same
gangs from which many asylum seekers are fleeing.[152]

By February 2020, the United States had deported more
than 250 Hondurans and Salvadorans, including children and
families, to Guatemala under the Guatemalan ACA.[153] Asylum
seekers deported to Guatemala under the ACA have reported
abusive treatment by U.S. border officials. These individuals
seeking protection at our borders have received no opportunity to explain to U.S. officials why they fled their home
countries and no meaningful access to counsel—in short, no
opportunity to apply for asylum:

> A Salvadoran man said that a US Department of Home-
> land Security official told him "there is no asylum" and
> there are no Central Americans allowed into the United
> States. Two women [deported to Guatemala] showed
> Refugees International evidence of abuse by domestic
> partners—pictures of physical injuries from brutal beat-

ings and a copy of a protective order from a court in El
Salvador—that they said U.S. officials at the border refused to let them present in support of their claims of fear
of return there.[154]

U.S. officials put the asylum seekers on planes to Guatemala
without telling them where they were going; they landed without knowing what country they were in.[155] There they waited
on the tarmac for hours, sometimes with small children, with
no food, water, or medical attention.[156] Then Guatemalan officials told the deported asylum seekers that they had 72 hours
after arrival to either begin the process of seeking protection
there or accept "voluntary return" to their home country of
Honduras or El Salvador.[157]

The Guatemalan asylum system is unfit to protect those
fleeing persecution. Access to asylum in Guatemala is very
limited: the country has only three officers who interview
applicants for asylum.[158] A recent Georgetown Law Human
Rights Institute report reveals protection gaps in Guatemala's
Migration Code, significant departures from the law in practice, and a general lack of capacity to handle an influx of asylum
claims.[159] The report raises serious questions as to how DOJ
and DHS could have reached the conclusion that Guatemala
provides "access to a full and fair procedure for determining
a claim to asylum or equivalent temporary protection," as required by the U.S. Immigration and Nationality Act.[160] It documents the lack of institutional capacity to prioritize asylum
and finds that the country is too dangerous for asylum seekers
to secure durable solutions there. "We're not a safe country,"
said Nery Rodenas, director of the Office of Human Rights of
the Archbishop of Guatemala. "If we have violence and people have to leave because they're going to get killed, this is not
a safe country."[161] "Asylum is not a priority for our country,"
according to the Guatemala Office of the Ombudsman.[162] As
a result, only 2 percent of those deported to Guatemala under

the ACA apply for asylum there; of the nearly 950 asylum seekers transferred in the first year of implementation, none were granted asylum.[163] Most "return to El Salvador and Honduras despite their fear of persecution there."[164]

Neither the texts of the ACAs nor the public announcements of them from the Trump administration denominate them as "safe third-country" agreements. Yet the administration officially classifies them that way, likely to justify their legality under the provision of the Refugee Act that permits removing a person under a bilateral agreement if the attorney general determines that the receiving country is one where the person's life or freedom would not be threatened on account of one of the five grounds. This provision also, of course, requires that the receiving country provide "a full and fair procedure" for applying for asylum or equivalent protection.[165]

The U.S. attorney general made a determination that Guatemala's asylum system was full and fair, based on the text of Guatemala's migration code and "representations by Guatemalan officials in exchanges with the U.S. State Department . . . that Guatemala has a competent immigration authority with clear procedures for addressing initial asylum applications."[166] The attorney general apparently did not consider whether the migration code was being implemented effectively or whether the "representations" of "Guatemalan officials" were adequate and true.

Whether the Guatemalan ACA is valid depends, therefore, on whether the attorney general's determination, based largely on the vague and conclusory "representations" of the Guatemalan government,[167] had a sufficient grounding in reality or whether the claims of nongovernmental observers and American public officials regarding the inadequacy of Guatemala's refugee adjudication processes more accurately reflect the facts on the ground.[168] It also depends on whether the returnees' lives or freedom would be at risk on account of one of the five grounds in Guatemala, a likely situation for those fleeing one of the transnational gangs that operate throughout Guatemala, Honduras, and El Salvador.

In early 2020, the ACLU, the National Immigrant Justice Center, the Center for Gender and Refugee Studies, and Human Rights First filed a lawsuit challenging the ACA in federal court in Washington, DC.[169] The litigation remains in very early stages; no decision has yet been issued.

Demolishing Asylum Screening: PACR and HARP

From its earliest months in office, the Trump administration decried the high proportion of asylum seekers who proved a credible fear of return.[170] Even after TCTB was initiated, ruling out credible fear for asylum seekers entering from Mexico, asylum officers sometimes made positive reasonable fear findings. Asylum seekers who established reasonable fear became eligible for hearings before immigration judges, and because of limitations on detention space, many families and others were released until those hearings could take place. In late 2019, the Trump administration was still looking for a way to circumvent an expedited removal process that resulted in temporary releases rather than immediate expulsion.

To enable even speedier removals, in late 2019 DHS established two new, extremely expedited versions of expedited removal, whereby the credible fear interview (CFI) is conducted while the asylum seeker is still in CBP custody and as early as within 24 hours of being apprehended.[171] These programs are called Prompt Asylum Claim Review (PACR) for non-Mexican asylum seekers in expedited removal proceedings and the Humanitarian Asylum Review Process (HARP) for Mexicans.[172]

According to DHS, those placed in PACR/HARP are generally transferred from the "hielera" (frigid CBP holding cells) to a 1,500-bed "soft-side" Border Patrol facility (a large tent),[173] although some individuals reportedly undergo the entire process while in the "hielera."[174] The individual is not transferred to ICE custody, as prior guidance mandated.[175] Families and adults in the CBP holding cells "frequently report being provided inedible or insufficient food and water, lack of basic sanitation, and inability to sleep because of overcrowding, lack of adequate bedding, cold, and lights that are kept on all night."[176]

At a designated time within 48 hours of being apprehended,[177] the individual is given 30 minutes to an hour to call family members, friends, or an attorney.[178] Even if the individual is able to contact an attorney, the attorney does not have any physical access to the CBP facility to interview the client in person, in contrast with the access attorneys typically have in ICE detention facilities.[179] Phone access following this initial call period is atypical.[180]

As soon as possible after the passage of 48 hours from the time of apprehension or earlier if the asylum seeker waives the consultation period, an asylum officer conducts a credible fear or reasonable fear interview by phone.[181] Requests for extensions are granted only in extraordinary circumstances.[182] If the asylum seeker has managed to secure an attorney, the attorney is permitted to connect to the interview by phone.[183] However, in practice, it is rare that an attorney manages both to speak to the client before the interview and to be present at the interview.[184]

An individual who receives a negative finding can seek a telephone review from an immigration judge.[185] The immigration judge review occurs quickly, as DHS aims to complete the process within no more than ten days.[186] Court documents in pending litigation indicate that such individuals generally remain in CBP custody for five to seven days,[187] far longer than the 72-hour maximum dictated by long-standing DHS policy.[188] If the immigration judge's review is unsuccessful, the individual is summarily deported. An individual with a positive finding is transferred to ICE custody.[189]

Along with the other exclusionary programs and bars, PACR and HARP have restricted access to asylum. As of late February 2020, DHS processed at least 1,200 people through PACR.[190] But in contrast to the other policies, such as regular expedited removal and MPP, DHS has not been even remotely transparent with the public regarding PACR and HARP. Reliable statistics on the numbers of asylum applicants affected are unavailable. What is known, however, is that the percentage of asylum seekers found to have credible fear fell dramatically, with most applicants receiving negative credible fear decisions.[191] The programs have been so successful at keeping asylum seekers out of the United States that they contributed to the decreased use of the MPP program.[192]

In late 2019, nonprofit legal providers challenged the legality of PACR/HARP in federal court, principally arguing that it conflicts with the statutory right to apply for asylum, abrogates the statutory and regulatory rights to consult with counsel before and during credible fear proceedings, and is an arbitrary and capricious change of policy.[193] The Immigration and Nationality Act states that all individuals placed in the credible fear process "may consult with a person or persons of [their] choosing prior to the interview or any review thereof."[194] The implementing regulations clarify that the chosen consultant also "may be present at the interview."[195] In addition to this right to consult, there is a right to retained counsel in both the Immigration and Nationality Act and Administrative Procedures Act that arguably applies to credible fear proceedings.[196] Plaintiffs in the lawsuit argue that the design and practice of PACR/HARP render access to counsel and consultation either impossible or not meaningful because of the short time frame, the lack of physical and telephonic access to CBP facilities, and the outright prohibition on attorneys' physical presence at interviews.[197]

Plaintiffs argue that PACR/HARP deprives asylum seekers, who have a statutory right to apply for asylum, of meaningful

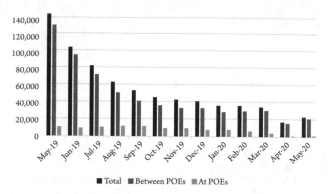

Figure 4.3 Arrivals at the U.S. Southern Border, May 2019–May 2020

Sources: U.S. Customs and Border Protection, Southwest Border Migration FY2018, https://www.cbp.gov/newsroom/stats/sw-border-migration/fy-2018; Southwest Border Migration FY2019, https://www.cbp.gov/newsroom/stats/sw-border-migration/fy-2019.

Note: POE = port of entry

access to protection by giving them little opportunity to articulate their claims. According to the plaintiffs, PACR/HARP is arbitrary and capricious in violation of the Administrative Procedures Act because it departed from long-standing policy without a reasoned explanation and did not consider the consequences of the change.[198] On November 30, 2020, the District Court agreed with the Trump administration that its PACR/HARP programs were lawful and granted summary judgment in favor of the government. The plaintiffs have appealed.[199]

The bottom line is clear: the combined effects of the 2019 policies—Remain in Mexico, Mexican National Guard enforcement on the Mexico-Guatemala border, the Third Country Transit Bar, the Asylum Cooperative Agreement with Guatemala, and PACR and HARP—effectively shut down access to asylum on the southern border, even before the administration piled on with expulsions purportedly justified by the COVID epidemic and a new, omnibus regulation to end asylum. As figure 4.3 shows, the number of migrants trying to enter the United States through the southern border declined dramatically, from over 144,000 in May 2019 to under 37,000 in January 2020. With the next two initiatives, the Trump administration put the final nails in the asylum coffin.

COVID-19 Expulsions

When two migrant children died in CBP custody in 2018, President Trump's chief adviser on immigration, Stephen Miller, argued that an obscure health law should be used to shut the border.[200] Miller continued to propose invoking this health law in connection with mumps and flu outbreaks in 2019, but it was not until the arrival of the coronavirus that he met with success.

On March 20, 2020, the Trump administration announced it would refuse entry to and immediately return practically all immigrants arriving at the U.S. border without valid documents for a period of thirty days to curtail the spread of COVID-19.[201] Vice President Mike Pence directed the Centers for Disease Control and Prevention (CDC) to issue this order over the objection of the CDC's director, Dr. Robert Redfield.[202] The order applied to all persons crossing into the United States through Canada or Mexico, regardless of their country of origin, who would otherwise be processed at a port of entry or Border Patrol station, namely, immigrants without valid documents or those inadmissible for other reasons.[203] U.S. citizens, lawful permanent residents, and valid visa holders are exempt by virtue of their admissibility, and there is an additional exception based on humanitarian and public safety considerations.[204]

To justify the policy, the order cites the risk of COVID-19 spread from Mexico and Canada and the danger of crowded conditions and lack of medical care at ports of entry and Border Patrol processing stations. The order discusses the spread of COVID-19 in Mexico and Canada,[205] and states that inadmissible immigrants crossing into the United States from those countries typically spend several days at ports of entry or Border Patrol stations waiting to be screened.[206] Although there were measures in place for addressing the risk of COVID-19 prior to the order, such as quarantining and testing symptomatic individuals, the order argues that the risk of exposure—among immigrants, from immigrants to staff, and vice versa—during processing time is too great for these measures to suffice.[207] It also states that there are no medical services whatsoever at more than half of the Border Patrol stations,[208] and it concludes that the immediate return of all inadmissible immigrants to their countries of origin was necessary.[209] The order was to last for thirty days, subject to modification or extension,[210] and has since been extended indefinitely.[211]

On March 24, 2020, the CDC issued an interim final rule retroactively conferring legal authority to the March 20 CDC order and modifying existing regulations to give the Trump administration the authority to implement it.[212] The order and interim rule are rooted in Section 362 of the Public Health Service Act, a little-known provision that authorizes the secretary of health and human services, in consultation with the president, "to prohibit, in whole or in part, the introduction of persons and property from such countries or places as he shall designate" and "for such period of time as he may deem necessary" if there is a serious danger that a communicable disease in those countries will be "introduc[ed]" into the United States absent restrictions.[213] Section 362 also authorizes the secretary of health and human services to issue regulations and apprehend, detain, or release individuals in order to prevent the "introduction, transmission, or spread" of a communicable disease.[214]

Because the prior regulations implementing these statutory provisions were limited, the CDC made three important modifications to the regulations through the interim rule. First, the new regulations clarify that CBP can go beyond quarantining and isolating people to actually suspending entry.[215] Second, they give CBP authority to physically return people to their countries of origin rather than simply refusing entry.[216] Finally, they clarify that any person from any country of origin passing through Canada and Mexico can be barred under the order, even if there is no formal determination of COVID-19 exposure in that country.[217]

Although neither the order nor interim rule specifically addresses how the policy applies to asylum seekers, subsequent CBP internal guidance and reporting reveal that all asylum seekers are barred from entry subject to very limited exceptions. The internal guidance, leaked to the media, instructs CBP officers to screen all arriving immigrants and, if inadmissible, immediately transport them to the nearest port of entry to return them to Mexico or Canada, depending on where they entered and regardless of whether they are from another country.[218] The only exception articulated in the guidance is that if the inadmissible immigrant *affirmatively* raises a fear of *torture*, and the CBP officer and his supervisor find the fear to be "reasonably believable," the individual is to be referred to an asylum officer for a credible fear or reasonable fear interview.[219] The absence of any other exceptions indicates that articulating a fear of persecution or a request for asylum or withholding of removal would not suffice, even though withholding of removal is mandatory under U.S. law for people whose life or freedom would be threatened in the country to which the person would be removed.[220]

Public health experts urged the secretary of health and

human services to withdraw the order "enabling mass expulsion of asylum seekers."[221] According to these leading experts, "the CDC order is based on specious justifications and fails to protect public health." These experts recommended that U.S. officials use evidence-based public health measures to process asylum seekers at the border.

Also, in connection with the coronavirus but with regard to asylum seekers waiting in Mexico under MPP, all MPP hearings scheduled through July 20 were postponed, but individuals were still required to report to ports of entry on their previously established court dates to get new hearing dates.[222] On July 17, 2020, DHS and DOJ announced that MPP hearings will resume only after these conditions are met: California, Arizona, and Texas move to Stage 3 of their reopening plans; the U.S. Department of State and the CDC lower their global health advisories, particularly with respect to Mexico; and Mexico lowers its health advisories for all Mexican border states.[223] COVID-19 cases have been reported in the largest Mexican encampment of some 2,000 asylum seekers waiting for their immigration court hearing.[224]

As figure 4.4 shows, in contrast with the lack of transparency with respect to PACR and HARP data, CBP regularly updates statistics on what it calls Title 42 COVID-19 "expulsions."[225] In the last third of March 2020, CBP removed more than 7,000 people seeking safety at the southern border by applying the new policy. That number steadily climbed to over 61,000 for the month of October 2020. As the COVID removals increased, processing in the normal course of immigration enforcement declined significantly, from over 23,000 border apprehensions in March to fewer than 1,200 in April and 1,600 in May. A similar decline occurred with respect to the number of people CBP determined to be inadmissible at ports of entry: from about 4,000 in March to some 400 in April and 1,000 in October 2020.

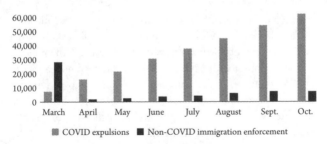

Figure 4.4 CBP COVID-19 Expulsions and Non-COVID-19 Immigration Enforcement at the U.S. Southern Border, 2020

Source: U.S. Customs and Border Protection, Nationwide Enforcement Encounters: Title 8 Enforcement Actions and Title 42 Expulsions, www .cbp.gov/newsroom/stats/cbp-enforcement-statistics/title-8-and-title-42 -statistics.

The human cost of this expulsion policy has been dire. DHS has started to detain families with children in an immigration jail more than 100 miles from the U.S.-Mexico border in Karnes, Texas, prior to expelling them.[226] In addition to expelling families with children—including newborn U.S. citizen children—by October 2020, DHS had removed more than 8,800 unaccompanied children under the CDC order, some as young as ten years old; in November 2020, a federal district court enjoined further expulsions of such children.[227]

Among those removed under the CDC order were political opponents of President Daniel Ortega of Nicaragua, whom U.S. secretary of state Pompeo calls a "dictator" who "doubl[es] down on repression," "imprisons pro-democracy activists," and "tramples human rights."[228] That did not prevent the Trump administration from deporting some 100 political opponents of Ortega via the COVID expulsion order.[229] One of the deported Nicaraguan activists was Valeska Aleman, who had been arrested and tortured before fleeing to the United States. When she asked a CBP officer to allow her to show evidence of her persecution to an asylum officer in a credible fear interview, the agent purportedly told her that "we don't do credible fear interviews anymore."[230] In violation of an agreement with Mexico, CBP has expelled non-Mexican children with no accompanying adult to Mexico to fend for themselves.[231] The acting CBP commissioner acknowledged that such expulsions violate the accord with Mexico, but officials nevertheless carried them out.

COVID removals are the fastest removal process CBP uses, averaging about 96 minutes.[232] The number of family members encountered along the southern border by Border Patrol agents declined from 84,486 in May 2019 to 972 in May 2020. Border inspectors encountered only 73 family members at the ports of entry in May 2020, down from 4,101 in May 2019.[233] Given this decline, a major demographic shift has occurred. More than 29,000 of the 32,500 individuals encountered by CBP officers in June 2020 were single adults, most of whom were Mexican.[234]

Immigration experts decried the COVID removals, pointing out that they are "designed to accomplish under the guise of public health a dismantling of legal protections governing border arrivals that the Trump administration has been unable to achieve under the immigration laws."[235] They also argued that the program is illegal. The legislative history of the statute, which originated in 1892, showed that as originally drafted, it would have allowed the president to suspend the immigration of infected foreign nationals. But Senator William Vilas complained that the provision would discriminate against people from other countries, and it was eliminated in favor of language in the current law that permitted the government to suspend the introduction of a communicable disease—without any authority to apply the suspension of admission only to foreign nationals or to deport such persons (rather than quarantine them).[236] The COVID-19 expulsion program applies only to foreign nationals; it exempts U.S. citizens and permanent residents arriving from Mexico, even if they are equally likely to be infected by the virus. It also exempts foreign nationals coming to the United States for purposes of commerce. So the program, as applied primarily to asylum seekers, is arguably beyond the power that Congress delegated to public health authorities.

A second issue is that Section 362 was last enacted in 1944, but several human rights statutes were enacted later. These include the Refugee Act of 1980, the Trafficking Victims Protection Reauthorization Act of 2008 (which provides special protections for unaccompanied child migrants), and the Foreign Affairs Reform and Restructuring Act (which prohibits deporting anyone to a country in which they are likely to be tortured). Applying the "last-in-time" rule of statutory interpretation—namely, that a statute inconsistent with an earlier statute is the one that controls—immigration advocates argue that the public health law must be applied consistently with the later laws. Harmonizing them would allow CBP to detain both citizens and foreign nationals, on a nondiscriminatory basis, for a period of testing and possible quarantine, but the government could not simply remove all foreign nationals based on the 1944 law.[237]

On September 11, 2020, the Trump administration issued a final rule to further buttress its power to expel anyone who had come from a designated foreign country "for such period of time that the Director deems necessary to avert the serious danger of the introduction of a quarantinable communicable disease."[238] The final rule clarifies that this new authority applies not only to persons at the border but also to those found anywhere in the United States.[239] The rule claims to override any "law" (e.g., the Refugee Act) that would otherwise authorize such persons to remain in the United States. American citizens and lawful permanent residents are exempted, however, even if they actively carry the disease. The final rule also clarifies that this CDC authority applies only to the "quarantinable" communicable diseases listed as such by the federal government.

The Trump administration had already issued another proposed rule in July 2020 to greatly expand its expulsion and removal authority in connection with infectious diseases in other countries. Purportedly justified on "national security" grounds, this proposed rule, finalized in December 2020 and effective January 22, 2021, would bar not only asylum but also nonrefoulement (withholding of removal) protection to anyone who is from or traveled through a country where an infectious disease is prevalent.[240] Moreover, as critics have observed, the bar would apply to those screened at the border, so that such asylum seekers could be immediately deported and would never have an opportunity to present their persecution claim to an immigration judge.[241] Such a sweeping rule could be used not only as a restriction during the current pandemic but also whenever there is an outbreak of any kind of infectious disease in another country.

More than 170 public health and medical experts urged the Trump administration to withdraw the "sweeping new bans" because the proposed rule "ignores and misuses the science and core principles of public health."[242] These experts also objected to the rule's grant to DHS and DOJ—"agencies that lack public health expertise—authority to label asylum seekers as a national security threat, scapegoating them as vectors for a potentially vast array of diseases, and denying them protection."[243]

THE END OF ASYLUM

Trump officials aiming to destroy the Refugee Act of 1980 were not satisfied with their exclusionary policies at the southern border or their many new procedural requirements and substantive restrictions that severely restricted asylum protections. In 2020, the administration went full throttle in its efforts to eviscerate a system that the five previous Republican and Democratic administrations had all implemented in accordance with the Refugee Act.

The Omnibus Asylum Rule

While litigation continued against each of the administration's exclusionary policies, the Trump administration was likely aware that some or all of them might ultimately be struck down by the courts or that a successor administration might repeal the administration's policies. To deliver a coup de grâce against the asylum system, the administration proposed a new rule in June 2020 and issued it as a final rule in December, after Trump was defeated in his effort to win re-election. Unless rescinded by the Biden administration through a new rulemaking procedure or nullified or permanently enjoined by the courts, this new rule will destroy the asylum system. It codifies some of the Trump administration's restrictive policies, as discussed in chapters 3 and 4, thereby making it more difficult for a future administration to restore the asylum system. In many respects, the new rule goes even further than the Trump administration's previous efforts to deport asylum seekers back to their persecutors. As discussed below, the new rule has many parts, each of which restricts the rights of asylum seekers. On January 8, 2011, a federal court temporarily enjoined implementation of the rule, as described below. But unless a federal court or the Biden administration eliminates the rule permanently, it will effectively end asylum in the United States.[1]

Imposing Bars to Asylum in Credible Fear Interviews

Until the new rule was issued, asylum officers conducting credible fear interviews were instructed that "evidence that the applicant is, or may be, subject to a bar to asylum or withholding does not have an impact on a credible fear finding."[2] The new rule imposes the opposite outcome: "The asylum officer shall take into account . . . the applicability of any bars to being able to apply for asylum or to eligibility for asylum set forth [in the Refugee Act], including any bars established by regulation."[3] The latter phrase pertains, in particular, to the Third Country Transit Bar (TCTB) discussed in chapter 4.[4] The Trump administration applied that bar starting in July 2019 to deny findings of credible fear to Central Americans and others who came to the United States through Mexico, but it had no specific regulatory authority to do so. The new rule provides explicit direction to exclude from the asylum process virtually all Central and South Americans as well as asylum seekers from around the globe entering the United States at its southern border.

Elimination of the Right to Testify at a Hearing

The regulation confirms fears that the government was aiming to eliminate the right of asylum seekers to testify at their hearings, as discussed in chapter 3.[5] It provides that either at the written or oral request of DHS, or at the judge's own discretion, an immigration judge who determines that an asylum seeker's written application has not established a prima facie claim may summarily deny asylum, withholding of removal and protection under the Torture Convention. The judge "need not conduct a hearing."[6] Because many asylum applicants, particularly those in detention, do not have lawyers and do not know, without professional counseling, what facts they must allege in their written applications to constitute a "prima facie claim," this provision alone will deny many asylum applicants a day in court. Without the chance to respond to questions from the judge that might enable them to demonstrate a well-founded fear of persecution, genuine refugees will be denied asylum under this new rule.[7]

Political Opinion Must Be Directed against a Government

A well-founded fear of persecution on account of political opinion is recognized by the Refugee Act as a basis for asylum. Nothing in the law requires that such a political opinion be directed against a state official or institution. Shortly before the new rule was published, in a case in which a Salvadoran woman had resisted the violence of a gang member, the Federal Court of Appeals for the Second Circuit had found that "resistance to the norm of female subordination to male dominance" is a political opinion.[8] In response to that decision, the new regulation slams the door on all political persecution claims based on "opposition to criminal, terrorist, gang, guerilla, or other nonstate organizations," unless the victim was persecuted or threatened for expressing opinions in favor of law enforcement by the government.[9]

Making Victims of Domestic and Gang Violence Ineligible for Asylum

As noted in chapter 3, Attorneys General Sessions and Barr and acting Attorney General Rosen certified cases to themselves in order to establish that asylum could rarely be granted on the basis of persecution by a spouse, domestic partner, or gang member.[10] The Trump administration decided to embed its opposition to domestic violence and gang claims into this regulation. The rule directs asylum officers and immigration judges to deny asylum on the basis of "interpersonal animus in which the alleged persecutor has not targeted, or manifested an animus against, other members of an alleged particular social group in addition to the member who has raised the claim."[11] This language is of a piece with the administration's prior and subsequent efforts to frame persecution by nonstate actors as private criminal activity that does not fit within the asylum framework.

This regulation also drastically changes the standard applied to domestic and gang violence claims in another way. Previously, to deny asylum based on the bar for internal relocation, a judge or asylum officer had to determine that, under all the circumstances, it would be reasonable to expect the applicant to relocate internally. The new rule establishes a presumption that internal relocation would be reasonable unless the applicant establishes that it would be unreasonable. Furthermore, under prior law, the adjudicator considered only the evidence of the hardships and threats that the applicant would experience in the applicant's own nation. Under the new regulation, when evaluating the possibility of *internal* relocation, the adjudicator must take into account the fact that the applicant was able to flee to the United States, as if the fact that the asylum seeker was not killed before escaping showed that the risk was not genuine.[12]

Ending Gender-Based Claims

Sessions's *A-B-* decision sought to eliminate domestic violence asylum claims by asserting that categories such as "El Salvadoran women who are unable to leave their domestic relationships where they have children in common with their partners" did not meet the definition of a particular social group. In the wake of this ruling, some female applicants claimed to be members of the social group "women" in their countries and argued that their domestic abusers had attacked them because of their gender. The Court of Appeals for the First Circuit seemed to accept this argument in *De Pena-Pan-iagua v. Barr*.[13] The regulation reverses *De Pena-Paniagua* and any similar cases by declaring that immigration courts "will not favorably adjudicate" asylum claims of persecution "based on . . . gender."[14] This part of the regulation contravenes years of official recognition of these cases, dating back to the 1995 *INS Gender Guidelines*, discussed in chapter 2, as well as international guidance from the Office of the UN High Commissioner for Refugees.

Female victims of domestic abuse have often supported their claims with published reports and written and oral testimony from experts who demonstrated that, particularly in the Northern Triangle countries, violence against women was endemic because many men have learned to view women as property, to beat them for disobedience, and to rape them. Experts and published reports also showed government failure to protect women from domestic and gang violence due to gender bias.[15] Immigration judges took this evidence into account in determining that persecution of the women was societally sanctioned rather than the result of a particular man's domination. To prevent judges from even considering such expert evidence, the new rule provides that "evidence offered in support of [an asylum] application which promotes cultural stereotypes about a country, its inhabitants, or an alleged persecutor, including stereotypes based on . . . gender, *shall not be admissible* in adjudicating the application" (emphasis added).[16] Judges, apparently, are directed to refuse to let an expert testify as to these matters.

Persecution on account of a victim's sexual orientation has

been recognized as a basis for asylum for thirty years.[17] These aspects of the rule may prevent grants of asylum in such cases in the future, however, because applications for protection against persecution based on sexual orientation or gender identity may be viewed as gender-based claims.[18] In addition, expert opinion on levels of homophobia within a country may be excluded from evidence as a result of the rule.

Death Threats No Longer Qualify as Persecution

Until publication of the new regulation, DHS trained its asylum officers to understand that "serious threats made against an applicant may constitute persecution even if the applicant was never physically harmed."[19] Federal Courts of Appeals have agreed.[20] But the new rule reverses that law, stating that "persecution does not encompass . . . threats with no actual effort to carry out the threats, except [for] particularized threats of severe harm made by an identified entity."[21] Apparently a person who is threatened with death should survive at least one attempted murder before seeking refuge in the United States or at least know the name of the person or "entity" that made an "immediate and menacing" threat.

Torture by Certain Public Officials is Not Torture

The provisions of U.S. law that implement the UN Convention Against Torture protect individuals fleeing harm that does not meet the asylum definition. They also protect refugees who are ineligible for asylum for a technical reason such as the Third Country Transit Ban.[22] Until the rule was issued, the Convention Against Torture's protection was extended to individuals fearing torture at the hands of government officials, such as police officers or jailors. It did not matter whether a higher official had ordered the government official to torture the victim.

The new rule, however, divides torturing officials into two categories: those who are acting "under color of law" and those who are not. Torture at the hands of officials in the latter category no longer qualifies as torture: "Pain or suffering inflicted by a public official who is not acting under color of law shall not constitute pain or suffering inflicted by or at the instigation of, or with the consent or acquiescence of, a public official acting in an official capacity."[23]

Therefore, a person fearing torture at the hands of an official, such as a police officer, who could not establish that the officer was acting under "color of law", would not be protected and would face deportation and renewed torture. Ironically, the new rule was issued just as the United States was undergoing a cataclysm of protest against the 8-minute torture and death of George Floyd at the hands of a police officer who acted in disregard of the Minneapolis Police Department's rules for the use of force. Perhaps that officer would be regarded as not acting "under color of law" under the definition of pain and suffering established by the rule, so the torture of Floyd would not be torture at all.[24]

Expanding Discretionary Denials

As noted in chapter 1, a person who is otherwise eligible for asylum could still be denied based on the adjudicator's "discretion." Discretionary denials have historically been rare, largely because of *Matter of Pula*, a case in which the applicant had entered the country with a fraudulent visa.[25] The Board of Immigration Appeals (BIA) held that though irregular entry was a negative factor that could have an impact on discretion, "the danger of persecution [if the applicant were deported] should generally outweigh all but the most egregious of adverse factors."[26] Pula was granted asylum.

Just in case an asylum seeker was able to establish eligibility for relief despite all the new bars and restrictions, the new rule seeks to overturn *Pula* by specifying several new discretionary factors that would justify denying asylum and deeming them "significant."[27] One such factor—the one in *Pula* itself—is unlawful entry or attempted entry into the United States, a factor that would apply to the thousands of people who cross the land border without authorization each year.[28] Another such factor is the applicant's not having sought asylum in a country of transit before entering the United States, an expansion of the consequences of the Third Country Transit Ban from those crossing the southern border to all applicants, including some of those who obtain visas to come to the United States and arrive by air, having passed through a third country en route.[29]

Several other new factors weigh even more negatively than those that are "significant." Immigration judges are told, for example, not to exercise discretion in favor of someone who spent more than fourteen days in another country en route to the United States without seeking asylum there or who transited through more than one country, regardless of how much time was spent in each one.[30] In "extraordinary circumstances, such as those involving national security or foreign policy," an immigration judge might grant asylum even if one of these factors was present; but even then, "a showing of extraordinary circumstances might still be insufficient to warrant a favorable exercise of discretion."[31]

Expanding the Firm Resettlement Bar

At least since 1980, the firm resettlement bar applied only to an asylum seeker who had "received an offer" of permanent resident status, citizenship, or some other type of permanent status in another country.[32] Even with such an offer, the bar did not apply if the asylum applicant had been in that country for a brief time while arranging to come to the United States, or if the country had substantially restricted the applicant's access to basic human needs.[33] The new regulation bars applicants who "could have" applied for and obtained an offer of "nonpermanent but indefinitely renewable" legal immigration status in a country through which they passed, even if they did not apply for such status or receive an offer. The new regulation also shifts the burden of proof on this issue, imposing it on the applicant rather than the government. It is not clear how applicants could disprove assertions that they "could have" obtained an offer for renewable status that they did not in fact receive. In addition, an applicant who voluntarily lived for a year or more in another country where she was not persecuted or tortured is barred, even without an offer of immigration status from that country.[34]

Violating Confidentiality

Prior law required DHS to keep the information in asylum applications confidential, to protect asylum seekers' families who remained in the applicants' countries. A persecuting government might retaliate against those family members if it were to learn that an applicant was complaining that the government had violated their human rights.[35] The new rule provides, however, that such information "may be disclosed as part of an investigation or adjudication of the merits of that application."[36] It delineates no limits on the persons to whom the information may be disclosed, so DHS or State Department employees may apparently ask officials of an allegedly persecuting government whether its police or military really did detain and beat an asylum seeker because of that person's political beliefs. Such an inquiry could put the applicant's family and friends at serious risk, which is why previous administrations took great care to keep asylum applications confidential.

As if asylum had not already been sufficiently nailed into

its coffin before the new rule was proposed, its promulgation as a final rule welds the cover to the casket. The significance of the sweeping new restrictions was not lost on the public. More than 87,000 comments were filed, overwhelmingly in opposition,[37] and the union of asylum officers took the extraordinary step of publicly opposing their agency's action, terming it "the most extreme in a recent series of draconian changes to the American asylum process," one that "dismantles . . . America's position as a global leader in refugee assistance."[38] As one director of an asylum clinic stated immediately after she read the proposed rule, "I cannot think of a single client I have represented in nearly 15 years as an immigration attorney who would meet these stringent new requirements."[39]

On January 8, 2021, three days before it would have gone into effect, the omnibus regulation was preliminarily enjoined by a federal court.[40] The basis for the court's decision was that acting DHS Secretary Chad Wolf had never been properly installed as acting secretary, so he had no authority to issue the regulation. As the court explained, when DHS Secretary Kirstjen Nielsen left office in 2019, the succession rules in effect at the time should have placed Christopher Krebs, the department's director of cyber security and infrastructure security, in the position of acting secretary. But Trump tweeted that Kevin McAleenan, the commissioner of border protection, was to be acting secretary, and McAleenan then purported to serve in that job. He ultimately designated Wolf to be his successor. But since McAleenan was in the job unlawfully, he had no authority to do so, and like McAleenan, Wolf had no legitimate power to issue regulations. The court's decision followed conclusions in four other cases that had similarly invalidated immigration regulations that DHS had issued after Nielsen's departure.[41]

In its last few days in office, the Trump administration made a final, desperate effort to make effective the omnibus regulation as well as others, such as the TCTB regulation, that DHS had issued during McAleenan's and Wolf's purported tenures as acting secretary. On January 11, 2021, three days after the court enjoined the omnibus rule, Wolf resigned as acting secretary, citing what he claimed were the erroneous court rulings that had questioned his authority. He remained an agency employee, however. As he made his way out of the secretary's office, Wolf designated Peter Gaynor, the administrator of the Federal Emergency Management Agency, as next in succession.[42] At the same time, he asked Gaynor to "ratify" all of the official acts that Wolf had undertaken, including the issuance of several immigration regulations such as the omnibus rule. Gaynor refused, but he delegated Wolf, who remained a DHS undersecretary, to exercise certain powers, including the power to "ratify any prior regulatory actions" of the department.[43] Pursuant to that delegation, Wolf purported to ratify his own previous attempts to issue the omnibus rule and other restrictions on immigration and asylum. With only hours remaining in President Trump's term in office, the Department of Justice asked the court to reconsider its preliminary injunction, based on Wolf's designation, Gaynor's delegation, and Wolf's self-ratification.[44] Whether this bootstrapping effort would succeed in court remained to be seen.

The Eleventh-Hour Deluge

As the fall of 2020 approached, the Trump administration continued to build on top of its omnibus rule and its prior appointments, decisions, and policy changes, further ensuring the complete destruction of the asylum system. The administration spent the last months of 2020 embedding as many roadblocks as possible in the way of a successor administration that might desire a more functional asylum system—one in line with the Refugee Act of 1980.[45]

Turning the Asylum Application Form into a Trap
for Migrants

For decades, the asylum application form has been difficult but not impossible for applicants to complete.[46] It required disclosure of a great deal of the applicant's personal history and a general statement of the reasons why the applicant feared being forced to return home. The applicant was invited to attach evidence to corroborate the allegations of persecution or threats of persecution; but applicants, who often completed the form online without the benefit of attorneys, were not required to explain a legal theory justifying decisions in their favor.

Simultaneously with its issuance of the omnibus regulation the Trump administration proposed to change the form and its instructions to require applicants to delve into legal theory.[47] Unless the use of the new version is enjoined by a court or changed by the Biden administration, one new question will ask, "If you are claiming membership in a particular social group, identify the particular social groups." This question is a trap. First, as explained above, the definition of what qualifies as a social group has been the subject of BIA and federal appellate court decisions for nearly forty years, and the ins and outs of social group definitions are the subjects of dozens of pages of small print in immigration and asylum textbooks. A person unfamiliar with this large body of law is very likely to make a mistake responding to this question and to describe a social group that some adjudicator believes does not qualify. (Recall that another of the Trump administration changes would allow judges to deny asylum without an oral hearing if the application documents do not show a basis for granting it.)

A second trap lies in a new question about causation: "You must explain why you believe the harm, mistreatment or threats you experienced were on account of one or more of the protected grounds." Sometimes, a persecutor's motive is easy to describe, such as where a police officer tells a person in custody that "I'm torturing you because you criticized our president." But more often, the persecutor's motive must be inferred from the conduct of the individual engaging in the persecution or, quite often, the conduct of similarly situated individuals over a long period of time, such as where a regime's military often arrests members of a dissident group. Collecting that information may require months of research and is not necessarily something that is known to the applicant on the day of filing the application. In addition, the nature of causation, like the definition of a social group, is the subject of dozens of judicial opinions.

Third, the new form incorporates several questions whose answers would likely disqualify the applicant under the omnibus regulation, such as "Did you or any member of your family included in the application transit through more than one country between your or their country of citizenship, nationality, or last habitual residence and the United States?"[48] Finally, the form has many lengthy questions that are so technical and convoluted that even many lawyers would have a hard time parsing them.[49]

New Judges

In July 2020, Attorney General William Barr appointed still another forty-six immigration judges in addition to the sixty-nine judges that the Trump administration appointed in 2018.[50] Nineteen of them had been lawyers for Immigration and Customs Enforcement (ICE), another ten had been state or federal prosecutors, and seven others had prosecution experience in the military. If any of the forty-six had ever represented an immigrant, their official biographies did not mention that fact.[51] Given their prior experience, these new judges are more

likely to view asylum cases from the perspective of the attorneys working for ICE rather from the vantage point of a neutral adjudicator. As explained in chapter 3, prior prosecutorial
experience correlates closely with lower asylum grant rates.

New Appellate Procedures

In August 2020, the Trump administration published yet another new proposed rule, this time to change the procedures
of the BIA so that the officials could more easily deny asylum.
First, the rule reduced the amount of time allowed to asylum
applicants to file a brief after receiving a copy of the transcript
of their immigration court hearing. Second, it limited applicants' ability to seek a BIA remand based on new evidence.
Most important, it would allow an immigration judge whose
decision had been reversed by the BIA to appeal the reversal
to the Executive Office for Immigration Review's executive
director, who then, using authority delegated by the attorney
general, could overrule the decision of the BIA and enter a
new decision that constituted a precedent. If made final, this
rule would probably mark the only instance in American law
in which a disgruntled lower court judge (in this case, one who
had denied asylum) could appeal a reversal by an appellate
judge.[52]

New Reasons to Reject Asylum Applications in
Immigration Court

In September 2020, the Trump administration published a
proposed regulation to force immigration judges to reject
more asylum applications.[53] The regulation, which was to become effective on January 15, 2021, provides that an application filed in immigration court is deemed incomplete if the
applicant does not "include a response to each . . . question"

or lacks required evidence described on the form and form instructions. For immigration courts, this rule would mirror the change that had been adopted by U.S. Citizenship and Immigration Services for affirmative applications a few months earlier.[54] Immigration courts are directed to reject such applications and return them to the applicant and to deem them "abandoned" if they are not corrected within thirty days. Abandoned applications would quickly be denied, resulting in orders of removal.[55]

This regulation will lead to many summary rejections, for several reasons. First, the application form asks several questions that an asylum seeker might reasonably leave unanswered, such as the question about the applicant's middle name, which, as explained in chapter 3, applicants typically leave blank if they have no middle name. Second, DHS has coded its online form so that, while applicants might try to comply with the requirements by entering the word "none" in a particular field that was inapplicable, the field will accept only numerical entries.[56] Third, the instructions require supporting evidence to be filed with an application.[57] Many applicants file their applications without supporting evidence, either because they do not yet have attorneys who could amass it or because they are up against the one-year deadline for filing an asylum application.[58] These applicants are then able to make use of the time between filing their application and their asylum hearing to gather supporting evidence, which they submit just before their hearing. Compiling massive amounts of evidentiary support before filing is particularly challenging for detained applicants, because they lack the ability to collect declarations from witnesses abroad or from experts.

The Trump administration intended the omnibus regulation to do even more damage to the asylum system when combined with its other regulations. For example, one feature of the omnibus regulation provides that the government will

place asylum seekers who establish credible fear into hereto-
fore rarely used "asylum-only" hearings, which prevent the
asylum applicant from asking an immigration judge for relief
from removal based on other laws. But another regulation
proposed by the Trump administration a few months later
provides that a person in asylum-only proceedings may not
receive asylum unless that person files the lengthy asylum
application within 15 days after a scheduling hearing, rather
than within one year after entering the United States. This will
prove almost impossible for most recent border-crossers who
are just getting their bearings in the United States. This regulation was preliminarily enjoined on January 14, 2021, just
before it would have become effective.[59]

The administration followed this regulation with one that
imposed new bars to asylum for individuals who had committed
specified minor offenses, once again justifying the restrictions
on the attorney general's power to create new bars to asylum
that were "consistent with" the Refugee Act. The new rule prohibits asylum from being granted to a person convicted two or
more times of driving under the influence of alcohol (even if
the conviction was only for a misdemeanor) and conviction
of any drug possession offense other than a single marijuana
possession offense involving 30 grams or less.[60] In November 2020, a federal court enjoined this new regulation on the
ground that Congress had crafted bars to asylum for certain
particularly serious crimes, and that adding additional offenses
to the list of bars was not consistent with the Refugee Act.[61]

Historically, both ICE and an asylum applicant may submit
evidence to the immigration judge, whose role is to be a neutral arbiter of the case. The regulation that imposed a 15-day
application deadline for asylum seekers in "asylum only" proceedings also authorizes immigration judges presiding in removal hearings to introduce evidence of their own, in addition
to the evidence supplied by the parties.[62] In a removal hearing,

each party may object to evidence offered by the other side, and the judge can then decide whether the evidence is genuine and relevant. However, it is hard to understand how an asylum applicant can object to evidence introduced by the judge, because no neutral official would be present to accept such an objection. The regulation also encourages judges to reject evidence of human rights violations published by journalists and human rights organizations and to give greater weight to the official pronouncements of U.S. government agencies,[63] some of which may be slanted to support the policies or electoral prospects of an incumbent president.[64]

Additional Burdens for Expert Testimony

In many cases, both official government publications and reports published by nongovernmental organizations fail to discuss the very particular type of persecution that an applicant suffered, so the asylum seeker or her attorney must find a historian, political scientist, anthropologist, or other social scientist who has specialized knowledge that could help to corroborate an unusual claim of persecution. Immigration courts regularly qualify such persons as "experts," which enables them to testify about their expert opinion, as opposed to what they have personally seen or heard. For example, one of the authors supervised a law school clinic case in which the successful applicant had to prove that the ruling party in Moldova, a country whose language is written in Cyrillic characters, persecuted activists who sought to restore the Romanian language, with its Roman characters, as in pre-Stalinist times. No evidence of such persecution appeared in official reports, but an expert corroborated it. In another successful case, an expert corroborated that a particular curse hurled at the asylum applicant by a shaman was a threat to poison her, providing an explanation that was not discussed in published reports.

However, in September 2020, the BIA issued a decision that constituted a precedent discouraging immigration judges from entertaining expert testimony.[65] The decision does not make it literally impossible for asylum applicants to use experts to support their cases, but it demands a much greater degree of specific knowledge relevant to the facts of the case before a judge can credit expert testimony.

Making It Easier to Overturn Grants of Asylum

Attorney General Barr's decision in *Matter of A-C-A-A-*, discussed in chapter 3, introduced a new procedural twist to make it easier for the BIA to overturn an immigration judge's grant of asylum.[66] If an ICE attorney had agreed to a stipulation that established an element of the asylum seeker's claim (e.g., a stipulation that the asylum seeker was a member of a valid social group), the attorney general directed that the BIA "should not accept" the stipulation. The BIA must independently decide whether the applicant has proved every element of his or her claim, and it should remand the case to an immigration judge who, despite the time pressure imposed by the metrics, did not analyze and justify findings on each of those elements.

Giving Adjudicatory Authority to the Director of the Executive Office for Immigration Review

Asylum policies can be changed in three ways: by acts of Congress, new regulations, or decisions that constitute precedents that are rendered in individual asylum cases, either by the BIA or by the attorney general. Examples of policy changes made through decision-making are Attorney General Sessions's decision that makes it very difficult for domestic violence victims to win asylum and Attorney General Barr's decision that purportedly prevents most families from being considered as social groups.

On the day of the 2020 presidential election, the Trump administration finalized a new regulation, proposed and implemented temporarily a few months earlier,[67] to give the executive director of the Executive Office for Immigration Review (EOIR) the authority to make such decisions.[68] The new regulation enabled the executive director to decide appeals that the BIA had not decided within 90 days (or 180 days, in the case of a case that had been assigned to a three-member BIA panel). Even though the attorney general had intervened several times during the Trump administration to reverse BIA precedents of prior administration, the administration now determined that "given the other obligations on the attorney general's schedule," in the future, the executive director should be able to issue precedent-making decisions in appeals that the BIA had not quickly decided.[69]

Immigration advocates had objected to this new regulation on the ground that it further politicized the adjudication of asylum cases, pointing out that senior officials of EOIR such as the executive director were political appointees. EOIR dismissed this objection, claiming that even though appointed to their jobs by the attorney general, "none of EOIR's employees are political appointees," that "the fact that the Attorney General, who is a political appointee, appoints an individual to a position does not convert that position to a political position," and that "even if the Director position were filled by a political appointee, that fact alone would not render the individual a biased adjudicator."[70]

Even after being voted out of office, the Trump administration worked feverishly to impose additional burdens on asylum seekers. It finalized several asylum regulations, including the omnibus asylum-destroying regulation that it had proposed the previous June, which would become effective just days before President Biden's inauguration.[71] Moreover, it continued to propose new regulations.

Making Erroneous Denials of Asylum Harder to Correct

Under the press of a crushing caseload, immigration judges occasionally denied asylum because they misunderstood the facts or misinterpreted the law. The BIA also erred from time to time. The asylum applicant is permitted to make a motion to the judge or to the BIA, asking the decision maker to reopen or reconsider an allegedly erroneous ruling. DHS lawyers sometimes agree with the asylum applicant and join in the motion. A Court of Appeals had held that an asylum adjudicator deciding a motion to reopen had to accept facts in a sworn statement as true unless they were inherently unbelievable.[72] A new regulation, proposed in late November 2020, specifies that "allegations of fact contained in a motion to reopen or motion to reconsider are not evidence and shall not be treated as evidence and [even if asserted by counsel] shall not be accepted as true." Furthermore, even if DHS makes the motion jointly with the asylum seeker, "an immigration judge or the Board retains discretion to deny a joint motion or an unopposed motion if warranted."[73]

Making it More Difficult for Asylum Seekers to Obtain Lawyers

On the same day that the Trump administration proposed the regulation making it more difficult to fix erroneous denials, it proposed another new regulation that would make it more difficult for asylum seekers to obtain legal help. For many decades, immigration judges were permitted to reschedule hearings "for good cause" and they did so liberally to enable unrepresented asylum seekers to obtain legal representation. But because many asylum seekers were poor or had fled without being able to escape with their financial resources, and the need for representation vastly outstripped the supply of pro bono lawyers, judges often granted two or three month-long postponements to enable asylum seekers in removal proceedings time to try to obtain counsel. The new regulation would tie the judges' hands and make it much more difficult for asylum seekers to obtain lawyers—without whom they will be much less likely to prevail.[74] The regulation provides that a judge need not reschedule a hearing if the asylum seeker has had at least ten days' notice of it and has failed to obtain a lawyer during that period. Once an asylum seeker does obtain a lawyer, any rescheduling of a scheduled hearing on the claim for asylum "is strongly disfavored" and should be granted only for very limited reasons such as the lawyer's having to conduct a trial in another court. Even then, the rescheduling would be limited to 14 days.[75]

Brick by brick, Trump has erected a "wall" of executive branch regulations and policies that has prevented the vast majority of asylum seekers from finding safety in the United States. Only a careful and dedicated effort by the Biden administration and Congress can rebuild what the Trump administration has destroyed.

6

THE BIDEN ADMINISTRATION, CONGRESS, AND A NEW BEGINNING

When Senator Edward Kennedy, who introduced the Refugee Act in the Senate,[1] presented the conference committee's report on the bill to the Senate, he explained that "it is the intention of the Conferees that the Attorney General should immediately create a uniform procedure for the treatment of asylum claims filed in the United States or at our ports of entry. Present regulations and procedures now used by the immigration Service simply do not conform to either the spirit or to the new provisions of this Act."[2]

Senator Kennedy's description of "present regulations and procedures" rings true today. Despite Congress's best intentions, the U.S. asylum system has been under sustained attack from an administration that issued regulations, published executive orders, and adopted procedures that were at odds with the language and purpose of the Refugee Act. Congress provided the executive branch with some flexibility to design a fair and efficient asylum procedure. But the Trump administration abused the leeway that Congress afforded, destroying the U.S. asylum system under the pretense of procedural and substantive reforms. The Biden administration and Congress must once again take back the reins and guide the executive branch toward a process that will fairly implement America's obligation to provide safe haven for asylum seekers.

The American government should restore the promise of its legislation enacted to protect refugees and once again make it possible for people fleeing persecution and torture to seek protection in America.[3] President Biden's immigration platform suggests that his team will repudiate many of Trump's harsh asylum practices through executive branch action.[4] In addition, Senator Patrick Leahy and Representative Zoe Lofgren have proposed thoughtful statutory reforms to provide enduring protection to refugees.[5] We endorse many of their ideas and suggest additional changes that aim to restore the goals of the 1980 act and modernize the U.S. asylum system.[6]

Executive Branch Actions

We begin this chapter by describing the mechanisms through which the Biden administration should begin to reverse some of the damage inflicted by the Trump administration. First, it should adopt new policies and change current practices with respect to asylum restrictions administered by the Department of Homeland Security (DHS) and the Department of Justice (DOJ) that are not required by current laws or regulations. Second, the attorney general should issue new rulings to restore protections for victims of domestic violence and others. Third, the Biden team could start the cumbersome process of writing new regulations to repeal or modify those that were issued between 2018 and 2020.[7] Fourth, and most important, particularly in the early months of the new administration, it should withdraw many of the appeals that were filed by the Trump administration, thereby allowing injunctions against several of Trump's regulations to go into force, and it should settle other pending lawsuits to restore significant elements of the system as they existed during previous Republican and Democratic administrations, or even improve on them.

New Policies and Precedents

Some, but not all, of the Trump administration's changes could be reversed by executive branch actions without going through the arduous process of issuing new regulations, although just as a new statute would "embed" new rules in a way that a later administration could not change by regulation, only a new statute or new regulations would "embed" them in the law so as to make them less susceptible to another regression in a later administration. For example, an opinion of a new attorney general could displace an opinion issued by Attorney General Sessions, but it could be reversed by a later opinion or a later regulation. Nonetheless, adopting new policies and establishing new precedents is easier to accomplish and faster than issuing new regulations. These measures will not only reverse extremist restrictions but will help protect refugees in robust ways, at least during the term of the Biden administration.

New Policies

These first steps we describe could be accomplished as soon as the Biden administration takes office, through executive orders or directives from the new secretary of DHS.

The omnibus regulation. As one of its first initiatives to protect asylum seekers, the Biden administration should begin the process of rescinding the omnibus asylum-destroying regulation that the Trump administration issued in its final weeks, after the President had lost his bid for re-election. As discussed in chapter 5, this regulation closes off the possibility for asylum for virtually all applicants. The Trump administration left this regulation, with an effective date four days before the end of its term, as a legal time bomb aimed at sabotaging any effort by an incoming secretary of homeland security to implement the provisions of the Refugee Act.

As noted in chapter 5, a federal court granted a preliminary injunction against the regulation. The administration should consent to a final injunction against it. In addition, it should begin the process of sweeping it off the books by proposing a new regulation to restore the status quo ante and to clarify and simplify asylum law. For example, the Trump administration's omnibus regulation codifies the "social distinction" requirement that the Board of Immigration Appeals grafted onto the definition of a persecuted social group. A replacement regulation should eliminate this requirement, which does not appear in the Refugee Act.

Expedited processes: Credible fear, PACR, and HARP. The expedited removal process has been perverted by an administration bent on excluding legitimate asylum seekers. The Biden administration should reform the expedited removal process to restore its intentionally low screening standard that makes it less likely that the United States will mistakenly return a refugee to persecution.[8] In the words of then–Senate Judiciary Committee chairman Orrin Hatch, the Senate's floor manager for the Illegal Immigration Reform and Immigrant Responsibility Act of 1996, the 104th Congress "intended [the expedited removal process] to be a low screening standard for admission into the usual full asylum process."[9]

The Trump administration distorted the credible fear process, denying genuine refugees the opportunity to present their claims to an immigration judge.[10] It did so by changing the guidance for asylum officers in their training manual, and that training manual can be edited anew. The Biden administration should rehabilitate the instructions given for over twenty years to asylum officers conducting the credible fear interview, namely, that they cannot assess any bars to asylum or other restrictions, including internal relocation. This would return these interviews to the long-standing practice whereby the application of bars and restrictions, often complex and nuanced, are decided by immigration judges who can take the time to consider them carefully. The Biden administration's revised training manual should also instruct asylum officers to return to the practice of applying the law of the most favorable circuit, given that they cannot know where in the country the applicants will settle before lodging their applications for asylum in an immigration court.

President Biden's team should also implement improved quality control provisions for expedited removal processes suggested by Senator Leahy and Representative Lofgren, such as the recording and random audits of Customs and Border Protection (CBP) interviews and regular reports on expedited removal by the U.S. Commission on International Religious Freedom.[11]

The Biden administration should also should restore the two-decade-old practice whereby all credible fear and reasonable fear interviews were conducted by trained asylum officers, not CBP agents. Credible fear decisions should be made only by professionals who are well trained in asylum law and whose goals are both to protect refugees and to screen out those who are not genuine refugees. The first of those goals is far from the mission of CBP.

The administration should also end the excessively expedited removal systems called Prompt Asylum Claim Review (PACR) and the Humanitarian Asylum Review Process (HARP), through which the Trump administration conducted hasty credible fear interviews while asylum seekers were still in CBP border facilities.[12] That is not how previous Republican and Democratic administrations for some twenty years implemented the expedited removal statute as applied to asylum seekers. Individuals who claim to be victims of persecution or torture should be given a chance to rest, eat, and consult with pro bono or other lawyers before the interviews take place.

As President Biden has suggested, the administration should allow the Asylum Office to retain jurisdiction to grant asylum to migrants who received positive credible fear determinations, reducing the burden on the overcrowded immigration courts.[13]

Ending pushbacks: Migrant Protection Protocols, tent courts, and metering. No law *requires* the administration to push back asylum seekers at the southern border to wait for months in squalid and highly dangerous conditions in Mexico until they are called for immigration court hearings.[14] In fact, the litigation challenging the Migrant Protection Protocols (MPP) has argued that the policy is illegal. In January 2020, as a candidate, President Biden tweeted that "on day one I will eliminate President Trump's decision to limit asylum and end the MPP program."[15] The administration should not place one more asylum seeker into MPP.

That said, the administration will face the logistical challenge of bringing thousands of migrants forced to remain in Mexico pending their hearings into the United States.[16] The COVID-19 pandemic adds another layer of complication; public health protocols for basic sanitary measures such as masks and handwashing, in addition to a testing and quarantine plan, will need to be established. It will take time to process so many asylum seekers all at once, even if most of them will be released on bond or recognizance rather than detained until their hearings, and new migrants will of course arrive at the southern border in the meantime. Therefore, as a matter of logistics, the Biden administration will likely establish some type of triage system to allow those still waiting in Mexico for their hearings under the MPP program into the United States—where they should have been all this time.

More immediately, the administration should dismantle the makeshift immigration courts in tents along the border, restoring asylum applicants' access to legitimate hearings in the United States at immigration courts elsewhere in the country. President Biden should also put an immediate end to the process of metering, which he describes as "disastrous" because it "forces people seeking asylum to wait on the streets in often-dangerous Mexican border towns for weeks before they are permitted to apply," creating "a horrifying ecosystem of violence and exploitation, with cartels kidnapping, violently assaulting, and extorting migrants."[17] Border facilities should be enlarged to accommodate peak periods of migration rather than rejecting or postponing the entry of people desperate for protection and shelter.

Reforming detention practices. Detention of people who show that they have a fear of persecution if returned home is unwarranted and inhumane. Moreover, detention prevents asylum seekers from accessing a fair process. The Biden administration should issue a new policy that sets as a default the release from detention of asylum seekers who pass the screening test. Such individuals should be detained only if DHS demonstrates to a judge that they are a flight risk even with alternatives to detention calculated to ensure appearance or that they pose a threat to society or an individual.[18]

The Biden team should follow the suggestion in the Leahy and Lofgren bills that detained asylum seekers should be held in the least restrictive conditions possible, such as recognizance, community supervision, or bond. If detained, they should be entitled to regular custody redetermination hearings.[19] Those bills also generally prohibit the detention of several categories of vulnerable individuals, including primary caregivers, those with a serious mental or physical illness or disability, and those with limited English proficiency and insufficient access to meaningful language services. The prohibition would extend to individuals determined by an asylum officer or an immigration judge to have a credible fear of persecution or torture, to be experiencing severe trauma, or to be a survivor of torture or gender-based violence. Consistent with the Flores Settlement Agreement, children should never be incarcerated.

The Biden administration should make all these policy

changes as soon as it takes office. To monitor compliance with these policies, the Biden administration should require an annual report from Immigration and Customs Enforcement providing the number of asylum seekers detained, the reasons for and length of their detention, the financial cost of their detention, and why effective and much less costly alternatives to detention were not used.

Family separation. The Biden administration should institute a policy that generally prohibits the separation of parents or guardians from their minor children at any stage of immigration proceedings.[20] Children and their parents should not be detained. The "binary option" should be discarded as a matter of administration policy.[21] The attorney general should direct U.S. attorneys to refrain from criminally prosecuting asylum seekers, especially families, for unlawful entry. This provision is an important step in ensuring compliance with Article 31 of the Refugee Convention, which provides that asylum seekers should not be punished for unlawful entry.[22] Children should never be separated from their parents to deter other endangered people from fleeing as families to the United States.

The federal government, rather than lawyers for the families, should assume responsibility for finding the parents of the at least 666 children separated by the Trump administration who, as of this writing, had still not been reunited with their families. The Biden administration should also settle lawsuits filed by separated families, including administrative claims under the Federal Tort Claims Act, offering compensation as well as lawful immigration status to separated parents and children who have not yet received such status.

Asylum cooperative agreements. As President Biden promised in his campaign platform, he should terminate the asylum cooperative agreements, such as the one that the Trump administration used to "transfer" asylum applicants to Guatemala for consideration of their claims there.[23] These agreements themselves explicitly anticipate that either party might cancel them.[24] Consistent with the Refugee Act, the Biden administration should not sign any new agreements unless the nation cooperating with the United States has a well-functioning asylum adjudication system and is reasonably free of violence and human rights violations.

Pretextual expulsions justified by the pandemic. The Trump administration used the pretext of the COVID-19 pandemic to accomplish what it had long wanted: a closure of the border with Mexico, even to asylum seekers who did not have the virus or known exposure to the virus.[25] The border closure failed to stop or slow the epidemic in the United States, and it was inconsistent with the government's legal obligations under the Refugee Act and the Refugee Convention to provide access to the asylum process for those expressing fear of persecution in their home country or in Mexico.[26] Until the regulation permitting the turnbacks and expulsions is repealed, the Biden administration should decline to use it against asylum applicants and should instead protect them and others from the spread of COVID-19 through measures informed by evidence-based public health standards.

Fair adjudication processes. The Biden administration should take several steps to make the asylum adjudication processes fairer. It should begin by withdrawing the prior administration's new asylum application form, which changed long-standing practice. The new form placed an excessive burden on asylum seekers both substantively, by requiring them to describe the social group to which they claimed to belong, and procedurally, by rejecting applications in which the asylum seeker had left a field blank because she did not know the answer to a question or because the question was inapplicable.[27]

As the authors and other experts on the asylum system have explained for many years, a fair asylum process requires more resources.[28] Staffing levels at the asylum office and the immigration court must be sufficient to ensure that asylum adjudicators can handle peak caseloads; can have sufficient time to review the documents carefully; can take thorough testimony from the applicant; and, in the case of immigration judges, can craft accurate and detailed decisions. In our prior research with asylum officers, they reported that decreases in the amount of time they were able to devote to adjudication negatively affected their ability to decide cases fairly.[29] This intuition has been scientifically supported through other empirical work.[30] The current immense case backlogs both at the asylum office and immigration courts further demonstrate the perils of insufficient resources for hiring adjudicators.[31] The immigration courts have been notoriously understaffed for decades in both judges and support staff, including law and administrative clerks.[32]

To create a professionalized and fair asylum process, the Biden administration must devote significantly more resources to the adjudication system.[33] President Biden should increase the number of asylum officers and allocate sufficient funds toward regular training for all asylum adjudicators.[34] In addition to providing more time for asylum officers to adjudicate cases, Congress should require that all asylum officers have a law degree. As reported in one of our previous studies, officers with a juris doctorate are able to adjudicate cases more quickly than nonlawyers, and we expect that these decisions are also more accurate given the increasing complexity of asylum law.[35] It should require human rights analysis by intelligence agencies and the State Department to present honest facts about conditions in other countries rather than soft-pedaling the harsh realities so that those reports would undercut asylum seekers' narratives.[36] The Biden administration should ensure that its asylum adjudicators receive detailed and relevant country conditions resources as required by regulation.[37]

The Biden administration should expand, professional-ize, and diversify the immigration courts and BIA. President Biden has urged a doubling of the current number of immigration judges.[38] We agree with this proposal. His administration should create an immigration bench that encourages the best immigration lawyers to become immigration judges. It should also establish diversity benchmarks to make the immigration courts more representative of U.S. society, including appoint-ing as judges immigrants who have naturalized, practitioners who have represented immigrants, and advocates from immi-gration nonprofits, among other groups. This is an important counterbalance to the Trump administration's appointment of immigration judges with law enforcement backgrounds. It should discontinue the "metrics" by which immigration judges' performance ratings are based on how quickly they decide cases, which discourages them from giving complex cases due consideration.[39] The Biden administration should improve its existing disciplinary process for immigration judges to ensure that it is rigorous, accessible to complainants, and fair.[40]

New Precedents

Victims of domestic violence and victims singled out because of family membership. A new attorney general should overturn the three decisions by Attorney General Sessions, Attorney General Barr, and acting Attorney General Rosen in *A-B-* and *A-C-A-A-* that made it extremely difficult for victims of domestic violence to win asylum. In fact, President Biden already made it clear that "under the Biden administration, the U.S. Depart-ment of Justice will reinstate explicit asylum protections—re-scinded by the Trump administration—for domestic violence and sexual violence survivors whose home governments can-not or will not protect them."[41] A new decision should also reverse the decisions through which the BIA has required victims of persecution because of their membership in a social group to prove that their social group is one that is regarded as "socially distinct" in their countries. A social distinction requirement does not appear in the Refugee Act, is inconsistent with earlier BIA precedents, and was expressly repudiated by the U.S. Court of Appeals for the Seventh Circuit.[42]

The DOJ should also reverse Attorney General Barr's decision to bar asylum for most victims of persecution on account of their family membership. This decision, too, flies in the face of long-standing precedent.[43]

Fair immigration court procedures. The new attorney general should reverse the decisions requiring immigration judges to deny release on bond to asylum seekers who have been found by asylum officers to have established a credible fear of persecution.[44] In addition, the attorney general should overturn the decisions that discourage expert testimony in immigration court cases,[45] allow immigration judges to order asylum seekers to be deported without giving them a chance to testify,[46] and direct judges to reject stipulations entered into by asylum seekers and DHS.[47]

New Regulations

The Biden administration should repeal many of the regulations put in place by the Trump administration by promulgating new regulations.[48] This is a longer-term solution, however, because the process of issuing new regulations, even if only to repeal unjust regulations, is cumbersome and could take a year or more. Once finalized, regulations can be subject to lengthy legal challenges.

Under the Administrative Procedures Act (APA), agencies have to provide "good reasons" for changing existing federal policy, respond to critical comments, and provide and engage with statistical and other empirical data, including

assessments of actions taken in light of the earlier regulation
or other societal changes.[49] The Supreme Court recently re-
affirmed long-standing law that agencies changing policies
must thoroughly and honestly engage with their earlier policy,
justify the change, and include assessments of changes made
in reliance on that earlier action.[50]

Courts might determine that rescission of the Trump administration's immigration regulations does not require justifications as elaborate as those that courts have demanded for
rescissions of government policies that had benefited indus-
tries or groups. The courts have often mentioned economic
reliance on those benefits as the reason to insist on full justifications for changed policies by a new administration.[51] In contrast, the Trump administration's asylum regulations are quite
new, and in any event, no individual or industry has relied on
them. They deny, rather than grant, benefits to asylum seekers,
so no asylum seeker, organization, or industry has an interest
in their perpetuation. The courts might therefore require less
justification for a Biden administration decision to jettison
such restrictions as the third country transit bar to asylum.
Of course, the Biden administration probably will not want to
risk having its regulations overturned, so it will likely decide to
elaborate why the Trump administration's policies are unjust
or too costly.

Drafting new regulations is a complicated, bureaucratic
process.[52] Once finalized, a final rule may be challenged
through litigation, which could take a year or more, and the
courts could ultimately send the agencies back to the drawing
board.[53] Nevertheless, seeking to short-circuit or circumvent
the usual rulemaking process is the one virtually sure way for
agencies to lose in court and have to start from scratch.

Despite these hurdles, unless reform legislation is politi-
cally feasible, the administration should quickly begin the process of using the APA to dismantle some of the regulations that

undermined the Refugee Act. The Biden team should start with repealing the omnibus regulation because it dismantles so many important aspects of the asylum process that the system can no longer be functional once it is in place.[54]

The Biden administration should then turn to the regulations that shut down access to asylum at the border, namely, the regulation that established the third country transit ban,[55] and the three regulations that use the COVID-19 pandemic as pretext to enable the expulsion of asylum seekers.[56] These are the interim final rule from March 2020 that enabled the Centers for Disease Control and Prevention to close the border and return asylum seekers to their home country regardless of whether there is a risk of COVID exposure in that country; the July 2020 proposed rule that would bar asylum to anyone who had traveled from a country where there was a risk of exposure to infectious disease; and the September 2020 final rule enabling the refusal of entry to and expulsion of asylum seekers based on the assessment by the centers' director of risk of spreading a "quarantinable communicable disease." Finally, the Biden administration should prioritize terminating the regulation that prevents asylum seekers from working lawfully for what may be years until their cases are heard, as this policy will cause tremendous hardship to genuine refugees.[57]

Once those regulations are dismantled, the Biden administration should change several other Trump-era rules to the extent that they have not yet been permanently enjoined. It should restore the integrity of its immigration adjudication system by eliminating the regulations allowing immigration judges to appeal BIA reversals of their decisions to the executive director of the Executive Office for Immigration Review and authorizing the executive director to have the power to decide appeals that the BIA has not completed within a unreasonably short time frame.[58] Second, it should dismantle two of the seemingly technical regulations that cause substantial

hardship to asylum seekers, namely, those that imposed fees
for asylum applications and applications from asylum seekers
for initial work authorization permits[59] and that require rejection of asylum applications in which the asylum seeker left
blank spaces for inapplicable information.[60] Finally, it should
eliminate the regulations imposing bars to asylum to applicants who crossed the border between official ports of entry,
which is currently enjoined,[61] or who had committed minor
crimes.[62]

Settling Pending Litigation

Perhaps most important, the new administration should
consider with great care the position it will to take in court
with respect to more than a dozen pending lawsuits that have
challenged the Trump administration's policies.[63] Rather than
continuing to defend the unfair practices that are being challenged in these suits, the government should withdraw pending appeals from injunctions that courts have entered against
its predecessor's unfair and illegal policies and, where appropriate, enter into consent judgments that restore fair rules for
processing asylum claims.

Settling litigation offers three great advantages for the
Biden administration, compared with writing new regulations.
First, this approach can cut years off the time it would take
to repeal or modify Trump-era regulations, because appeals
can be withdrawn or settlements negotiated in weeks. Second,
they are semipermanent, because although courts may modify consent agreements that they have entered, undoing them
over the objection of one of the parties is not easy, requiring
the agreement of the court in which the controversy was settled. The Flores Settlement Agreement of 1997, for example,
which prohibited the incarceration of migrant children who
were awaiting court hearings, has remained in force for more

than twenty years, despite efforts by the Obama administration to narrow it and by the Trump administration to persuade the court to vacate it.[64]

Third, by cooperating with the migrants' legal representatives, such as the American Civil Liberties Union, the Biden administration can craft consent judgments that effectuate its desired policies. For example, rather than risking the possibility that a court would uphold the omnibus regulation, the administration should agree that it is invalid and consent to a permanent injunction against it or a court decision vacating it.[65] Similarly, it could settle the *Las Americas v. Trump* case, in which several plaintiff organizations challenge the changes that the Trump administration made to the immigration court system.[66] A negotiated resolution of that case could be a vehicle for major procedural and structural reforms of that system.[67] In a relatively short period, therefore, the administration could achieve in court settlements important reforms that could take Congress quite some time to accomplish or that Congress might lack the votes to achieve.

In addition, as part of a settlement of the National Association of Immigration Judges' appeal of its decertification, the administration should withdraw the Trump administration's petition to decertify the association as a union and the public voice for the judges. The association has played a valuable role in increasing public awareness of the need for nonpolitical judgment of asylum cases.

Legislation to Restore Access to the Asylum Process

Any steps taken by the Biden administration to restore or improve the asylum process could be reversed by a later president. In addition, some of the changes that should be made could be accomplished only by legislation because they would require the revision of existing statutory law, the reorganizations of government functions, or the appropriation of funds. Finally, as noted above, changes that would need to be made by issuing new regulations could take years, but if Congress had the political will to do so, it could make those changes by legislation much more quickly, and because the legislative reforms would not curtail individual rights, they would not be subject to attacks in the courts.

Although the 2020 elections awarded control of both houses of Congress to legislators from the Democratic party, the filibuster remains a formidable obstacle to enactment of controversial legislation, such as laws expanding the rights of asylum seekers. Accordingly, our suggestions for legislative reform are in the nature of a long-term agenda, even if they cannot become law in the near future.

The starting point for creating a fair system for protecting asylum seekers are provisions in the Refugee Protection Act of 2019 bills discussed above that were sponsored by Senator Patrick Leahy and Representative Zoe Lofgren.[68] Changes in asylum law and procedure made by the Trump administration after those bills were drafted need to be addressed in legislation. We make specific suggestions below about how Congress should change the statute, including updating and improving the Lofgren and Leahy bills.[69] We described many of the needed changes above in connection with regulatory reform, but even if the Biden administration is able to achieve these objectives by executive action, they should be codified more permanently by legislation.

These legislative changes should restore and expand substantive standards and procedural protections in the asylum process. In addition to restoring the long-standing *Acosta* standard for the definition of social groups,[70] which focuses on immutable traits rather than the confusing "social distinction" and "particularity" requirements,[71] it is time for Congress to add persecution on account of gender identity and sexual orientation as a ground for asylum.[72] The law should be amended, as well, to make clear that applicants fleeing harm at the hands of a nonstate actor must show only that the authorities were unwilling or unable to protect them and that the persecutor could find them if they relocate within their country.[73] In other words, Congress should ensure that asylum seekers are not required to show that the government "sponsored" or was completely helpless to halt the persecution. In order to conform U.S. asylum law to international refugee law obligations, Congress should make asylum mandatory.[74] Congress should also repeal the section of the law that allows the attorney general to create additional bars to asylum; only Congress itself should have the authority to establish new exclusions to asylum protection.

On the procedural side, in immigration court, Congress should codify in a statute the requirement that immigration courts provide asylum applicants with the right to be present and testify orally at their removal hearings.[75] The authors have long recommended, and the Leahy and Lofgren bills include, a repeal of the one-year deadline for asylum applications, which causes applications to be rejected regardless of their merits and in ways that adversely affect women, LGBTQ+ applicants, and certain nationalities in particular.[76] In the expedited removal process, Congress should reinstate the appropriately low credible fear screening standard that enabled Republican and Democratic administrations to ensure that the United States did not return any refugee to persecution. Congress should also prohibit credible fear determinations while migrants remain in temporary CBP custody, a method used by the Trump administration to limit the opportunity for a fair interview. Finally, Congress should restore the long-standing prohibition on fees for asylum applications and initial employment authorization and should adhere to the decades-long policy for asylum application forms, ensuring that these forms cannot require applicants to set out their legal theories, such as a definition of their social groups.

Turning to Trump's border exclusions, Congress should also prohibit the new bars to asylum, those applying to persons who entered the United States between ports of entry, transited through other countries without seeking asylum, or committed minor crimes such as marijuana possession. Congress should mandate an end to the program of expelling asylum seekers simply because they came from countries in which diseases were present and should tighten the public health law that the Trump administration used to justify the expulsion of asylum seekers, with no evaluation of their claims, during the COVID-19 pandemic.[77] Congress should also repeal the section of the law on which President Trump relied to create the Migrant Protection Protocols, or in the very least make it clear that it cannot be applied to asylum seekers.[78]

Congress should require DHS and DOJ to keep accurate statistics in asylum cases, including statistics based on the full life cycle of cases as they move from the jurisdiction of one agency to another. Congress should also establish diversity goals and standards for the recruitment and hiring of asylum officers, immigration judges, and BIA members, ensuring that asylum adjudicators reflect the United States' diversity.

In addition, Congress should amend the statute to accomplish several reforms that the Biden administration cannot achieve alone. First, Congress should create a commission to study how the immigration courts and the BIA could be made independent of political influence, either by turning these bodies into an Article I court (a court created by Congress, like the Tax Court, that is not part of the federal judiciary) or by making the judges special magistrates of the federal district courts. The National Association of Immigration Judges and the American Bar Association, as well as many scholars, has long recommended this central feature of due process for litigants.[79] To help alleviate the million plus immigration court case backlog, Congress should authorize DHS asylum officers to evaluate all asylum claims in the first instance, not only those filed by affirmative applicants and unaccompanied minors.[80]

Congress should fund counsel for indigent asylum seekers before the asylum office and the immigration courts. Research shows that competent representation facilitates fair and efficient decision-making by immigration judges and that represented immigrants are far more likely to appear for their immigration hearings.[81] The Leahy and Lofgren bills would allow immigration judges to appoint counsel in all cases and require them to do so for children and other vulnerable applicants.[82] Similarly, the FAIR Proceedings Act, sponsored by Senator Kirsten Gillibrand, mandates the appointment of counsel for children and vulnerable immigrants—including the indigent and disabled along with survivors of abuse, torture, or violence—and allows the appointment of counsel in all cases.[83] We agree that children and other vulnerable applicants should be entitled to counsel at government expense, but beyond that the same test for indigence that is used in criminal cases should be applied to all asylum claimants. To ensure fairness and efficiency, counsel should be appointed in all cases in which that test is met, whether they are before the asylum office or the immigration courts. Congress should also devote resources toward ongoing know-your-rights presentations and other efforts to ensure that asylum seekers are educated about the processes both at the asylum office and the immigration courts.[84]

Robust judicial review is a key ingredient of a fair process. Congress should reinstate judicial review of discretionary decisions by immigration adjudicators, applying the abuse-of-discretion standard that existed before enactment of the 1996 act.[85] In particular, with respect to the asylum process, the federal courts should be able to review all discretionary determinations in asylum claims and all denials of applications for withholding of removal or protection under the Convention Against Torture.[86]

It may be impossible to locate the parent of every child separated by the Trump administration. But trying to do so is a government responsibility. Congress should not only ban such separations in the future but also authorize the appropriation of funds to DHS or the Office of Refugee Resettlement to conduct international searches for those who were deported. It should also create immigration relief for separated parents and children and provide them with funding for humanitarian support, such as psychological counseling for the toxic stress and trauma the Trump administration forced them to endure.

Congress should also authorize appropriations to build decent temporary housing for adults, families, and unaccompanied children during initial processing. These reception centers, like those in several European countries, should have safe, clean accommodations; healthy meals; appropriate hygiene; reasonable ambient temperatures; and emergency medical care where necessary. At the reception centers, asylum seekers should be given sufficient time to recover from their journeys before the asylum officer interviews them, and they should be able to meet with pro bono or private lawyers who could help prepare them for credible fear interviews. The shelters should be operated under the auspices of the Office of Refugee Resettlement in the Department of Health and Human Services, which is not a law enforcement agency but has experience in housing children in shelters and resettling adult refugees. Congress should authorize appropriations for case workers to help asylum seekers access social services and education provided by state and local governments and to make sure that they have information about required court appearances and transportation to the courts.

A New Beginning

By its last day in office in January 2021, when this book went to press, the Trump administration had nearly destroyed the U.S. asylum system through its harsh policies. The Biden administration and Congress should step in to revive and improve the asylum law that Congress established forty years ago. The Biden administration can and should make many improvements as quickly as it can, but they need to be buttressed in the longer term by Congress with a revamped asylum system that cannot be dismantled by an ill-intentioned executive branch. New policies and precedential decisions, new regulations, settlements in pending cases, and a new statute should return the United States to a leadership role in the global development of asylum law. Congress should also create an independent, professionalized asylum adjudication process. A new system must ensure that asylum hearings are fair and efficient and that they are administered by carefully selected and well-trained adjudicators with sufficient resources to make accurate and transparent decisions. Finally, Congress must eliminate arbitrary barriers to accessing the asylum process at the border.

It is time for the new Biden administration and Congress to recreate a refugee protection system that reflects the long-held American belief that the United States should be a safe haven for those who are forced to flee from persecution.

ACKNOWLEDGMENTS

The authors wish to thank Ahilan Arulanantham, William Buzbee, Lucas Guttentag, and Lisa Heinzerling for discussing key ideas with us. Many thanks to Austin Rose, Hana Kassem, David Blumenthal, Abigail Kelati and Heather Adamick for their excellent research assistance; Temple Law librarian Julie Randolph for speedy and outstanding research; and Josette Finnegan for her good-natured support. Thank you to Dean William Treanor of Georgetown Law School and Dean Gregory N. Mandel of Temple Law School for research funding and support that made this work possible. Many thanks to our spouses and children for their patience as we devoted long hours to this project.

NOTES

Introduction

The chapter epigraphs are from White House, *Remarks by President Trump on the Illegal Immigration Crisis and Border Security*, November 1, 2018, www.whitehouse.gov/briefings-statements /remarks-president-trump-illegal-immigration-crisis-border-se curity/; and @realDonaldTrump, Twitter, June 25, 2018, 8:43 a.m., https://twitter.com/realDonaldTrump/status/10112282 65003077632; see also U.S. Department of Justice, *Attorney General Jeff Sessions Delivers Remarks to the Executive Office for Immigration Review* (Oct. 12, 2017), www.justice.gov/opa/speech /attorney-general-jeff-sessions-delivers-remarks-executive-of fice-immigration-review.

1. Pub. L. No. 96–212, 94 Stat. 102 (1980).
2. "Although the right of asylum has been regarded as an historic tenet of American political policy, it has not been set forth in any statutory provision." Hearings on H.R. 2816 Before the Subcomm. on Immigration, Refugees and International Law of the House Comm. of the Judiciary, 96th Cong., 1st Sess., at 186 (1979); Edward M. Kennedy, *Refugee Act of 1980*, 15 *Int'l Migration Rev.* 141, 150 (1981): "For the first time, the new Act establishes a clearly defined asylum provision in United States immigration law."
3. Arthur C. Helton, *Political Asylum Under the 1980 Refugee Act: An Unfulfilled Promise*, 17 *U. Mich. J. L. Rev.* 243, 249–50 (1984), describing congressional frustration with executive branch failure to implement criteria, guidelines, or legislation for asylum,

"legislators introduced bills to require the INS to conform its standards and practices to those of the Protocol, applying a consistent steady pressure for change from 1973 until the passage of the 1980 Act"; Deborah E. Anker and Michael H. Posner, *The Forty Year Crisis: A Legislative History of the Refugee Act of 1980*, 19 *San Diego L. Rev.* 9, 11, 48 (1981); Kennedy, *Refugee Act*, 141, 144.

4. Convention Relating to the Status of Refugees, adopted July 28, 1951, 19 U.S.T. 6259, 189 *U.N.T.S.* 137, entered into force Apr. 22, 1954.

5. Kennedy, *Refugee Act*, 141, 142–43; Stephen H. Legomsky, *The Making of United States Refugee Policy: Separation of Powers in the Post–Cold War Era*, 70 *Wash. L. Rev.* 675, 682 (1995).

6. Jaya Ramji-Nogales, Andrew I. Schoenholtz, and Philip G. Schrag, *Refugee Roulette: Disparities in Asylum Adjudication*, 60 *Stan. L. Rev.* 295, 353 (2007).

7. "The right of asylum is in many ways the most basic of all human rights. This country was founded and was built on a promise to open doors to those who seek to escape persecution." Immigration Reform: Hearings Before the Subcomm. on Immigration, Refugees, and International Law of the House Comm. on the Judiciary, 97th Cong., 1st Sess. 621 (1981).

8. Adam B. Cox and Cristina M. Rodríguez, *The President and Immigration Law*, 119 *Yale L. J.* 458, 464 (2009).

9. See also Catherine Y. Kim, *The President's Immigration Courts*, 68 *Emory L. J. 1* (2018); and Fatma Marouf, *Executive Overreaching in Immigration Adjudication*, 93 *Tulane L. Rev.* 707 (2019).

10. The Federalist No. 51 (James Madison), at 322.

11. Cass Sunstein, *Constitutionalism After the New Deal*, 101 *Harv. L. Rev.* 421, 509 (1987): "In a period of executive ambivalence, checks may be an important instrument of statutory implementation."

12. J. R. DeShazo and Jody Freeman, *The Congressional Competition to Control Delegated Power*, 81 *Tex. L. Rev.* 1443, 1456 (2003).

13. Jack Beerman, *Congressional Administration*, 43 *San Diego L. Rev.* 61, 71–73, 77–82 (2006); Kennedy, *Refugee Act*, 141, 144, explaining that "one of the principal arguments for the [Refugee

Act of 1980] was that it would bring the admission of refugees under greater Congressional and statutory control."

14. Sunstein, *Constitutionalism*.

15. Id., at 485.

16. Id., at 428.

17. Id., at 485.

Chapter 1

1. U.S. Holocaust Memorial Museum, *The Evian Conference*, https://encyclopedia.ushmm.org/content/en/article/the-evi an-conference.

2. Reflecting on the Evian Conference forty years later, Vice President Walter Mondale recalled, "At stake at Evian were both human lives—and the decency and self-respect of the civilized world. If each nation at Evian had agreed on that day to take in 17,000 Jews at once, every Jew in the Reich could have been saved." See www.nytimes.com/1979/07/28/archives/evian-and-geneva .html.

3. Elliott Robert Barkan, *And Still They Come: Immigrants and American Society, 1920 to the 1990s*, 51 (New York: John Wiley & Sons, 1996).

4. Gordon Thomas and Max Morgan Witts, *Voyage of the Damned*, 2nd ed. (Stillwater, MN: Motorbooks International, 1994); Nicholas Day, *No Turning Back*, Washington Post (Aug. 26, 1998).

5. U.S. Holocaust Memorial Museum, *Postwar Refugee Crisis and the Establishment of the State of Israel*, Holocaust Encyclopedia, https://perma.cc/2VH5-NRG2.

6. United Nations Convention Relating to the Status of Refugees, adopted July 28, 1951, 19 U.S.T. 6259, 189 U.N.T.S. 137, (entered into force Apr. 22, 1954).

7. The UN Conference of Plenipotentiaries on the Status of Refugees and Stateless Persons adopted the Convention Relating to the Status of Refugees in July 1951. The treaty entered into force in April 1954; www.unhcr.org/en-us/5d9ed32b4.

8. Susan Martin et al., *The Uprooted: Improving Humanitarian*

Responses to Forced Migration, 31 (Lanham, MD: Lexington Books, 2005).

9. Id., at 34–35. The protocol was signed by the president of the U.N. General Assembly and by the secretary general in January 1967 and entered into force that same year. United Nations Protocol Relating to the Status of Refugees, opened for signature Jan. 31, 1967, 19 U.S.T. 6223, T.I.A.S. No. 6577, 606 U.N.T.S. 267, at Art. I (1-2) (entered into force Oct. 4, 1967; for the United States, Nov. 1, 1968) ("The States Parties to the present Protocol undertake to apply Articles 2 through 34 inclusive of the Convention to refugees hereinafter defined," omitting "as a result of events occurring before 1 January 1951" from the refugee definition).

10. Office of the U.N. High Commissioner for Refugees (UNHCR), *The State of the World's Refugees 2000*, 79–86, https://perma.cc /5AEB-GNXT.

11. Walter F. Mondale, *Evian and Geneva*, *New York Times* (July 28, 1979), www.nytimes.com/1979/07/28/archives/evian-and-ge neva.html.

12. "International resettlement, which had been taking place at the rate of about 9,000 per month in the first half of 1979, increased to about 25,000 per month in the latter half of that year. Between July 1979 and July 1982, more than twenty countries—led by the United States, Australia, France, and Canada—together resettled 623,800 Indochinese refugees." UNHCR, *State of the World's Refugees 2000*, 86.

13. Austin T. Fragomen Jr., *The Refugee: A Problem of Definition*, 3 *Case W. Res. J. Int'l L.* 45, 62–64 (1970).

14. Refugee Act of 1980, P.L. 96–212 (1980).

15. David A. Martin, *Symposium, Making Asylum Policy: The 1994 Reforms*, 70 *Wash. L. Rev.* 725, 728–29 (1995).

16. USA for UNHCR, *Refugees in America*, www.unrefugees.org /refugee-facts/usa/; Philip Connor and Jens Manuel Krogstad, *For the First Time, U.S. Resettles Fewer Refugees Than the Rest of the World* (July 5, 2018), www.pewresearch.org/fact-tank /2018/07/05/for-the-first-time-u-s-resettles-fewer-refu gees-than-the-rest-of-the-world/. In addition to a robust refugee

admissions program, the United States provided very significant assistance to refugees abroad and funded about one-quarter of UNHCR's regular annual budget. U.S. Department of State, *Refugee and Humanitarian Assistance*, www.state.gov/policy-issues /refugee-and-humanitarian-assistance/; Democratic Staff, Committee on Foreign Relations, U.S. Senate, *Global Forced Migration: The Political Crisis of Our Time* (June 18, 2020), https:// perma.cc/RB4P-KQLW.

17. Deborah E. Anker and Michael H. Posner, *The Forty Year Crisis: A Legislative History of the Refugee Act of 1980*, 19 *San Diego L. Rev.* 9, 41 (1981).

18. 8 U.S.C. 208(d)(1).

19. *Immigration and Naturalization Service v. Stevic*, 467 U.S. 407 (1984).

20. *Immigration and Naturalization Service v. Cardoza-Fonseca*, 480 U.S. 421 (1987).

21. The majority opinion held that if the applicant shows that in his "country of origin every tenth adult male person is either put to death or sent to some remote labor camp, . . . it would be only too apparent that anyone who has managed to escape from the country in question will have 'well-founded fear of being persecuted' upon his eventual return." *Cardozo-Fonseca*, at 431, quoting A. Grahl-Madsen, *The Status of Refugees in International Law*, 180 (Leyden: A. W. Sijthoff, 1966).

22. Susan Gzesh, *Central Americans and Asylum Policy in the Reagan Era*, Migration Policy Institute (Apr. 1, 2006), www.migra tionpolicy.org/article/central-americans-and-asylum-policy -reagan-era. "Characterizing the Salvadorans and Guatemalans as 'economic migrants,' the Reagan administration denied that the Salvadoran and Guatemalan governments had violated human rights. As a result, approval rates for Salvadoran and Guatemalan asylum cases were under 3 percent in 1984. In the same year, the approval rate for Iranians was 60 percent, 40 percent for Afghans fleeing the Soviet invasion, and 32 percent for Poles." See also Gil Loescher and John Scanlan, *Calculated Kindness: Refugees and American's Half-Open Door, 1945 to the Present* (New York: Free Press, 1986).

23. Gregg A. Beyer, *Reforming Affirmative Asylum Processing in the United States: Challenges and Opportunities*, 9 American Univ. Int'l L. Rev. 43, 59–60 (1994). Written by the then-director of the new Asylum Office, this article provides excellent context and analysis of the challenges during the early years of the corps and initial reforms to address the problems noted in the text.

24. *American Baptist Churches v. Thornburgh*, 760 F. Supp. 796 (N.D. Cal., 1991) (settlement decree). See 67 *Interpreter Releases* 1480 (1990).

25. 55 *Fed. Reg.* 30,674 (1990).

26. See 8 *C.F.R.* § 208.1(c) (1993); now 8 *C.F.R.* § 208.1(b).

27. David A. Martin, *Symposium: Making Asylum Policy—The 1994 Reforms*, 70 *Wash. L. Rev.* 725, 727 (1995).

28. Id., at 727–28.

29. 8 *C.F.R.* 208.9(b).

30. See Board of Immigration Appeals, *Immigration Review Function*, 48 *Fed. Reg.* 8038 (Feb. 25, 1983) (to be codified at 8 *C.F.R.* pts. 1, 3, 100). Before the 1983 creation of EOIR as an immigration review agency, immigration judges served at the INS. Initially called "special inquiry officers," the INS retitled them "immigration judges" in 1973. T. Alexander Aleinikoff and David A. Martin, *Immigration: Process and Policy*, 2nd ed., 107–9 (Minneapolis: West, 1991).

31. 8 *C.F.R.* 1003.10.

32. Jaya Ramji-Nogales, Andrew I. Schoenholtz, and Philip G. Schrag, *Refugee Roulette: Disparities in Asylum Adjudication*, 60 *Stan. L. Rev.* 295, 309 (2007). Until 2003, the prosecuting attorneys were INS employees. The Homeland Security Act of 2002 transferred them to Immigration and Customs Enforcement in the Department of Homeland Security.

33. 8 *C.F.R.* 1240.3.

34. *Matter of Pula*, 19 I. & N. Dec. 467 (BIA, 1987).

35. See Kate Aschenbrenner, *Discretionary (In)Justice: The Exercise of Discretion in Claims for Asylum*, 45 *U. Mich. J. L. Reform* 595 (2012), reporting only a handful of discretionary denials.

36. 8 *C.F.R.* 1240.12.

37. Gregg A. Beyer, *Reforming Affirmative Asylum Processing in the United States: Challenges and Opportunities*, 9 American Univ. Int'l L. Rev. 43, 49–52 (1994).

38. Martin, *Symposium*, 725, 732.

39. U.S. Immigration and Naturalization Service, news release, *Asylum Reform: 5 Years Later—Backlog Reduced and Number of Non-Meritorious Claims Drops* (2000), https://www.uscis.gov /sites/default/files/document/news/Asylum.pdf.

40. He complained that in 1992, he had been able to detain only 1,169 of the "15,000 'inadmissibles' who came through JFK." Ira Mehlman, *The New Jet Set: How Questionable Political Asylum Claimants Enter the U.S. at N.Y., New York's John F. Kennedy International Airport Without Any Difficulty, National Review* (Mar. 15, 1993).

41. Patrick Radden Keefe, *The Snakehead: An Epic Tale of the Chinatown Underworld and the American Dream* (New York: Doubleday, 2009).

42. Tim Weiner, *Pleas for Asylum Inundated System for Immigration, New York Times* (Apr. 25, 1993).

43. Martin, *Symposium*.

44. U.S. Immigration and Naturalization Service, *Rules and Procedures for Adjudication of Applications for Asylum or Withholding of Deportation and for Employment Authorization*, 59 Fed. Reg. 62, 284 (Dec. 5, 1994).

45. U.S. Immigration and Naturalization Service, *Asylum Reform*, 2.

46. Id.; Martin, *Symposium*.

47. U.S. Immigration and Naturalization Service, *Asylum Reform*, 2.

48. Id.. "This is further illustrated by comparing the cases approved in FY 1999: Only 19 percent of the pre-reform claims were approved while 44 percent of the post-reform cases were approved."

49. See Susan F. Martin and Andrew I. Schoenholtz, *Asylum in Practice: Success, Failures, and the Challenges Ahead*, 14 Geo. Immig. L.J. 589, 596–600 (2000).

50. See Memorandum from Phyllis Coven, Office of International Affairs, U.S. Immigration and Naturalization Service, *Considerations for Asylum Officers Adjudicating Asylum Claims from*

Women 3 (1995); Martin and Schoenholtz, *Asylum in Practice*, 589, 597–598.

Chapter 2

1. Div. C of Pub. L. 104-08, 110 Stat. 3009-46, enacted Sept. 30, 1996.
2. The full history of the legislative battle over these new restrictions is reported by Philip G. Schrag, *A Well-Founded Fear: The Congressional Battle to Save Political Asylum in America* (New York: Routledge, 2000).
3. The restriction appears at 8 U.S.C. Sec. 1158(a)(2)(B). One exception was for changed circumstances, such as a recent coup in the asylum applicant's country. The other was for "extraordinary" circumstances, such as an illness that prevented the foreign national from filling out the applicant form until more than a year had passed since entry into the United States. See 8 U.S.C. Sec. 1158(a)(2)(D) and 8 *C.F.R.* Sec. 208.4(a)(4) and (5). For an analysis of how the one-year deadline produces random results rather than decisions on the merits of claims, see Philip G. Schrag et al., *Rejecting Refugees*, 52 *Wm. & Mary L. Rev.* 652 (2010).
4. The implementing regulations itemize several types of situations, such as serious illness that would constitute extraordinary circumstances, and add that such circumstances "are not limited" to those in the list. 8 *C.F.R.* Sec. 208.4(a)(5), 1208.4(a)(5). But we are not aware of any case that has recognized lack of knowledge as an extraordinary circumstance.
5. A person who fails the screening test may appeal the screening decision immediately to an immigration judge employed by the Department of Justice, but if the judge does not overturn the decision, no appeal to a federal court is permitted. Lawyers are not permitted to represent applicants in the appeal to the immigration judge. 8 U.S.C. Sec. 1225.
6. See the discussion in chapter 1 of the *Stevic* case and the higher standard for granting withholding of removal as opposed to asylum.
7. U.S. Commission on International Religious Freedom, *Report on Asylum Seekers in Expedited Removal*, 6 (2005).

8. Congressional Research Service, *Immigration: U.S. Asylum Policy*, rpt. R45539 (Feb. 19, 2019), at 38, table B-3.

9. Department of Justice, *Designating Aliens for Expedited Removal*, 69 *Fed. Reg.* 48,877 (2004).

10. 8 U.S.C. Sec. 1158(a)(2)(A).

11. Government of Canada, *Final Text of the Safe Third Country Agreement* (2002; entered into force in 2004), https://perma .cc/6QJK-K7SB. In July 2020, the Federal Court of Canada ruled that the agreement was invalid under the Canadian Charter of Rights and Freedoms. *Canadian Council for Refugees v. Minister of Immigration*, docket IMM-775-17 (Fed. Ct. Canada, July 22, 2020), https://decisions.fct-cf.gc.ca/fc-cf/decisions/en/item/482 757/index.do. The Canadian government has appealed the decision.

12. See the discussion of the Asylum Cooperative Agreements in chapter 4.

13. 8 U.S.C. Sec. 1225(b)(1)(D) (bar on appeals); 1252(e)(5) (limitation on review through habeas corpus petitions); *Dept. of Homeland Sec. v. Thuraissigiam*, —U.S.__, 140 S. Ct. 1959 (2020).

14. 8 U.S.C. Sec. 1158(a)(3). In 2005, Congress slightly opened the door by allowing appeals for rejections based on the deadline where the rejection was based on a legal interpretation rather than a finding of fact. See Rebecca Sharpless, *Fitting the Formula for Judicial Review: The Law/Fact Distinction in Immigration Law*, 5 *Intercultural Hum. L. Rev.* 58 (2010).

15. 8 U.S.C. Sec. 1252(e)(3). Such a challenge was mounted by the American Immigration Lawyers Association, but the U.S. Court of Appeals for the District of Columbia affirmed a district court's decision upholding the law. *Amer. Immig. Lawyers Assn. v. Reno*, 199 F. 3rd 1352 (D.C. Cir., 2000).

16. 8 U.S.C. Sec. 1225(b)(2)(C).

17. See the discussion of the Migrant Protection Protocols in chapter 4.

18. 8 U.S.C. Sec. 1225(b)(i)(B)(ii), (b)(2)(A).

19. In Operation Compliance, for a sixty-day period, affirmative asylum applicants who lost before immigration judges in Hartford were immediately taken into custody pending appeals. Sharon A.

Healey, *The Trend Toward the Criminalization and Detention of Asylum Seekers*, 12 *Human Rights Brief* 1, 14 (2004).

20. See Congressional Research Service, *Expedited Removal of Aliens: Legal Framework*, Report R45314 26 (2019). For statistics on immigration detention and a description of the conditions of detention, see American Civil Liberties Union, Human Rights Watch, and National Immigrant Justice Center, *Justice-Free Zones: U.S. Immigration Detention Under the Trump Administration* (2020).

21. A port of entry is a facility at which a person may lawfully enter the United States. It is staffed by personnel who inspect entry documents such as passports and visas.

22. 8 U.S.C. Sec. 1226(a)(2)(A); 8 C.F.R. Sec. 236(d)(1). An "arriving alien," defined by 8 U.S.C. Secs. 1.1(q) and 1001.1(q) to include those "attempting to come into the United States at a port of entry," is not eligible for bond. *Jennings v. Rodriguez*, U.S. 138 S. Ct. 830 (2018). Oddly, therefore, asylum seekers who commit a misdemeanor by wading or rafting the Rio Grande to enter the United States are eligible to be released on payment of bond, without being subjected to other conditions such as having to wear ankle monitors or to report periodically to ICE offices, while those who seek to enter lawfully at a land border crossing are ineligible. From 2005 until 2019, asylum seekers who entered the United States other than at ports of entry, were put into expedited removal, and were found to have credible fear were deemed eligible for release on bond by an immigration judge. *Matter of X-K-*, 23 I. & N. Dec. 731 (BIA, 2005). In 2019, however, the attorney general ruled that *X-K-* was wrongly decided, and he overruled the decision. *Matter of M-S-*, 27 I. & N. Dec. 509 (A.G., 2019).

23. See Immigrant Legal Resource Center, *Representing Clients in Bond Hearings: An Introductory Guide* (2017), https://perma.cc/7RLA-LNJE; Matthew Ormseth, *Undocumented Immigrants Detained in Connecticut Face the Highest Average Bond in the U.S.*, *Hartford Courant* (July 30, 2018).

24. 8 U.S.C. Sec. 1226(a)(2)(B).

25. Alina Das, *No Justice in the Shadows*, 121 (New York: Bold Type Books, 2020).

26. Lauren-Brooke Eisen, *Inside Private Prisons: An American Dilemma in the Age of Mass Incarceration*, 145–49 (New York: Columbia University Press, 2018). The two companies were the Corrections Corp. of America (later renamed CoreCivic) and the GEO Group. Id.

27. Department of Homeland Security, *Approp. Act*, fiscal year (FY) 2010, Pub. L. 111–83 (Oct. 28, 2009). See also Denise Gilman and Luis A. Romero, *Immigration Detention, Inc., J. Migration and Human Security* 1 (May 2018), https://doi.org/10.1177%2F2311502418765414.

28. Michelle Ye Hee Lee, *Clinton's Inaccurate Claim That Immigrant Detention Facilities Have a Legal Requirement to Fill Beds, Washington Post* (May 15, 2015). The "bed mandate" was repealed in 2017, but the amount of detention space remained available, maintained by long-term contracts between ICE and the private prison corporations requiring ICE to pay them for making the beds available. Detention Watch Network, *Detention Quotas* (May 9, 2020).

29. 8 U.S.C. Sec. 1158(b)(1)(B)(iii). This provision was apparently added to the law to overrule cases such as *Mendoza Manimbao v. Ashcroft*, 329 F. 3rd 655 (9th Cir., 2003), which held that minor inconsistencies that are not pertinent to the essence of the asylum claim were not a basis for denial.

30. The provision is codified at 8 U.S.C. Sec. 1158(b)(1)(b)(ii). For an example of a denial based on such lack of corroborating evidence, see *Aden v. Holder*, 589 F. 3rd 1040 (9th Cir. 2009).

31. See Deborah Anker, Emily Gumper, Jean C. Han, and Matthew Muller, *Any Real Change? Credibility and Corroboration After the Real ID Act, Immigration and Nationality Law Handbook 2008–2009*, 357, 371.

32. See *Agbuya v. INS*, 241 F. 3rd 1224, 1228 (9th Cir., 2001); *Borja v. INS*, 175 F. 3rd 732, 734–36 (9th Cir., 1999) (en banc).

33. See H. Rept. 109–72, at 163 (2005). The new provision is codified at 8 U.S.C. Sec. 1158(b)(1)(B)(i).

34. U.S. Border Patrol, *Illegal Alien Apprehensions from Countries Other Than Mexico by Fiscal Year, FY 2000–FY 2017* (from 65,614 in FY 2004 to 154,987 in FY 2005).

35. Congressional Research Service, *Gangs in Central America* 2, RS22141 (May 10, 2005). The murder rate in Honduras was 45.9 per 100,000 people, compared with 5.7 in the United States. Id.

36. See Congressional Research Service, *Gangs*, at 2; Jose Miguel Cruz, *Central American Gangs Like MS-13 Were Born Out of Failed Anti-Crime Policies, The Conversation* (May 8, 2017), https://perma.cc/9YV3-7LQC.

37. The gangs sustained themselves by extortion, forcibly recruiting young boys to act as lookouts and drug runners. Many gang members also preyed upon young girls, sexually assaulting them with impunity and murdering those who refused their advances. Center for Gender and Refugee Studies, University of California, Hastings College of the Law, *Guatemala's Femicides and the Ongoing Struggle for Human Rights*, 8–9, 12 (2006), https://perma.cc/WV2K-YTNQ; KIND, *Neither Security Nor Justice: Sexual and Gender-Based Violence in El Salvador, Honduras and Guatemala*, 5–6 (2017), https://perma.cc/3PAR-X2WX.

38. About 8,000 non-Mexican children fled to the United States in FY 2005. Jacqueline Bhabha and Susan Schmidt, *Seeking Asylum Alone: Unaccompanied and Separated Children and Refugee Protection in the U.S.*, 1 J. of the History of Childhood and Youth 126, 134 (2008). But it is not possible to know how many came by themselves and how many were accompanied by a family member, because CBP did not keep separate statistics on the arrivals of "family units" until FY 2012. Congressional Research Service, *Immigration: Recent Apprehension Trends at the U.S. Southwest Border*, R46012, at 8 (Nov. 19, 2019). Starting in 2003, pursuant to a clause in the Homeland Security Act, children who arrived unaccompanied by an adult were transferred fairly promptly to the custody of the Office of Refugee Resettlement in the Department of Health and Services (HHS), which was able to place most of them in the physical custody of relatives, in foster homes, or in group shelters that were, for the most part, much more welcoming than jails. See Christopher Nugent, *Whose Children Are These? Towards Ensuring the Best Interests and Empowerment of Unaccompanied Alien Children*, 15 Boston Univ. Publ. Int'l. L. J. 15

(2006). The act did not provide for HHS custody of accompanied children, however. Until Hutto was converted from a prison to a family immigration detention center, the government had only a very small facility in Pennsylvania, with fewer than 100 beds, for the detention of migrant families. See Philip G. Schrag, *Baby Jails: The Fight to End the Incarceration of Refugee Children in America*, 190–91 (Berkeley: University of California Press, 2020).

39. See, e.g., Margaret Talbot, *The Lost Children*, New Yorker (Mar. 3, 2008).

40. *Bunikyte v. Chertoff*, case A-07-CA-64-SS (W. D. Tex., 2007).

41. Dora Schriro, *Weeping in the Playtime of Others: The Obama Administration's Failed Reform of ICE Family Detention Practices*, 5 J. on Migration and Human Security 452 (2017).

42. See INS, Board of Immigration Appeals, *Procedural Reforms to Improve Case Management: Final Rule*, 67 Fed. Reg. 54,878 (Aug. 26, 2002); Jaya Ramji-Nogales, Andrew I. Schoenholtz, and Philip G. Schrag, *Refugee Roulette: Disparities in Asylum Adjudication*, 60 Stan. L. Rev. 295, 353 (2007).

43. See Peter J. Levinson, *The Facade of Quasi-Judicial Independence in Immigration Appellate Adjudication*, 9 Bender's Immig. Bull. 1154, 1155–56 (2004); Stephen Legomsky, *Restructuring Immigration Adjudication*, 59 Duke L.J. 1635, 1668–69 (2010).

44. Ramji-Nogales et al., *Refugee Roulette*, 358–59.

45. CBP, *Designating Aliens for Expedited Removal*, 69 Fed. Reg. 48877 (Aug. 11, 2004). More stringent entry requirements already prevented the vast majority of asylum seekers without visas from flying to the United States to seek asylum. International Organization for Migration, *International Terrorism and Migration* 10–11, 14–18 (2010), https://perma.cc/M786-637T.

46. E.g., in FY 2008, the last full year of the Bush presidency, DHS completed 4,886 credible fear interviews and it found credible fear in 66 percent of the cases. During the Obama years, this percentage rose as high as 86 percent (in FY 2013). DHS, *Credible Fear Cases Completed and Referrals for Credible Fear Interviews*, FY 2016–18 (May 12, 2020).

47. See the discussion of the credible fear screening standards in chapter 4.

48. Obama was criticized by immigration advocates as the "deporter in chief" because removals reached record numbers during his administration; but before 2014, Obama prioritized removals of noncitizens with criminal histories and recent border-crossers who had no valid claim to remain in the United States. See Muzaffar Chisti, Sarah Pierce, and Jessica Bolter, *The Obama Record on Deportations: Deporter in Chief or Not?* Migration Policy Inst. (Jan. 26, 2017), https://perma.cc/TM8K-RPFG.

49. S. 744, Sec. 3401 (113th Cong.); Barack Obama, *Statement of Administration Policy: S. 744* (June 11, 2013), https://perma.cc/NJ7W-PHME. The bill passed the Senate but was never considered in the House.

50. *Matter of A-R-C-G-*, 26 I. & N. Dec. 388 (BIA, 2014), overruled by *Matter of A-B-*, 27 I. & N. Dec. 227 (A.G., 2018). As applied to asylum officers in credible fear determinations, *A-B-* was partially invalidated in *Grace v. Barr*, 965 F. 3rd 883 (D.C. Cir., 2020). In August 2020, the Trump administration filed a petition for a rehearing of the case by the full Court of Appeals.

51. World Bank, *Intentional Homicides: Honduras, 1990–2017*, based on statistics from the U.N. Office of Drugs and Crime.

52. Alan Gomez, *El Salvador: World's New Murder Capital*, USA Today (Jan. 7, 2016).

53. María Fernanda Pérez Arguello and Bryce Couch, *Violence Against Women Driving Migration from the Northern Triangle*, Atlantic Council (Nov. 8, 2018), https://perma.cc/8XTZ-BBW9.

54. Edward Alden, *Is Border Enforcement Effective? What We Know and What It Means*, 5 J. on Migration and Human Security 481 (2017).

55. U.S. Border Patrol, *Illegal Alien Apprehensions from Countries Other Than Mexico by Fiscal Year*, https://perma.cc/F5MG-MYHJ.

56. Congressional Research Service, *Unaccompanied Alien Children: An Overview*, R43599 (Oct. 9, 2019).

57. U.S. Border Patrol, *Southwest Border Sectors, Family Unit and Unaccompanied Alien Children (0–17) Apprehensions FY 14 Compared to FY 13*, https://perma.cc/84F6-KUZY.

58. The average daily population of migrants detained by ICE grew

from about 20,000 in FY 2005 to nearly 35,000 in FY 2013. U.S. Conference of Catholic Bishops and Center for Migration Studies, *Unlocking Human Dignity: A Plan to Transform the U.S. Immigrant Detention System* 7 (2015), https://perma.cc/8TC3 -QB86.

59. For the history of these projects, see Schrag, *Baby Jails*, 115–47.
60. *Flores v. Meese*, 828 F. 3rd 898 (9th Cir., 2016).

Chapter 3

1. *Full Text: Donald Trump Announces a Presidential Bid, Washington Post* (June 16, 2015).
2. Josh Dawsey, *Trump Derides Protections for Immigrants from "Shithole' Countries, Washington Post* (Jan. 12, 2018).
3. "Remember that speech I made [referring to Mexicans as "rapists"] and I was badly criticized," Trump said at a rally. "Turned out I was a hundred per cent right. That's why I got elected." Susan B. Glasser, *Trump's Cynical Immigration Strategy Might Work for Him—Again, New Yorker* (June 22, 2018).
4. A total of 85,000 refugees were admitted into the United States in fiscal year (FY) 2016. In FY 2017, a partial year for the Trump presidency, the number dropped to 53,700. In FY 2018 and 2019, the numbers were 22,500 and 30,000. Pew Research Center, *Key Facts About Refugees to the U.S.* (Oct. 7, 2019), https://perma .cc/B55D-K2QP. For FY 2020, the State Department planned to admit only 18,000 refugees, and for FY 2021, only 15,000. For FY 2020, U.S. Department of State, *Refugee Admissions*, https:// perma.cc/PV3S-JYRC; for FY 2021, U.S. Department of State, *Transmission of the President's Report to Congress on the Proposed Refugee Admissions for Fiscal Year 2021*.
5. 8 *C.F.R.* Sec. 1003.1(h)(1).
6. Attorney General Sessions used this self-referral authority nine times in his first year in office alone. In contrast, President Obama's attorneys general self-referred only four cases in eight years. Sarah Pierce, *Sessions: The Trump Administration's Once-Indispensable Man on Immigration, Migration Information Source* (Nov. 8, 2018), www.migrationpolicy.org/article/sessions-trump-administra tions-once-indispensable-man-immigration.

7. Today's forced migrants often flee nonstate persecutors who target them for social group characteristics connected to gender, sexual orientation, age (children), and family. See Andrew I. Schoenholtz, *The New Refugees and the Old Treaty: Persecutors and Persecuted in the Twenty-First Century*, 16 *Chicago J. Int'l Law* 81, 92–119 (2015).

8. *Matter of A-B-*, 27 I. & N. Dec. 316 (A.G., 2018). The Attorney General's analysis relied on the *M-E-V-G-* decision, in which BIA added these two additional prongs (particularity and social distinction) to the long-standing "common immutable characteristic" definition of a particular social group. *Matter of M-E-V-G*, 26 I. & N. Dec. 227 (BIA, 2014).

9. *Matter of A-R-C-G-*, 26 I. & N. Dec. 388 (BIA, 2014).

10. U.S. Citizenship and Immigration Services, *RAIO Directorate—Officer Training, Definition of Persecution and Eligibility Based on Past Persecution* 28 (rev. Feb. 21, 2012), https://perma.cc/U4P8-9SYM.

11. U.S. Citizenship and Immigration Services, *RAIO Directorate*.

12. *Matter of O-Z- & I-Z-*, 22 I. & N. Dec. 23, 26 (2013).

13. *Grace v. Whitaker*, 344 F. Supp. 3rd 96 (D.D.C. 2018). The district court's decision applied only to DHS's screening decisions. The court could not bind the Department of Justice's immigration judges or the Board of Immigration Appeals because negative asylum decisions by immigration judges can only be appealed to BIA and then to U.S. Courts of Appeals and are not subject to district court review. 8 U.S.C. Sec. 1252. But the reasoning of Judge Sullivan's statutory interpretation applies as well to final decisions on the merits of asylum cases, and at least one Court of Appeals, has found it persuasive, declaring that *Grace* "abrogated" *A-B-*. *Antonio v. Barr*, 959 F. 3rd 778 (6th Cir., 2020).

14. *Grace v. Whitaker*, 344 F. Supp. 3rd 96, 126 (D.D.C., 2018), affirmed in part and reversed in part by *Grace v. Barr*, 965 F. 3rd 883 (D.C. Cir., 2020).

15. *Grace v. Barr*, 965 F. 3rd 883 (D.C. Cir., 2019).

16. Id.

17. *Matter of A-C-A-A-*, 28 I. & N. Dec. 84 (A.G., 2020).

18. Id. at 90, 91 n. 4.

19. Id. at 90.

20. In Barr's words, "For instance, the immigration judge did not cite any evidence that the respondent's parents themselves had ever said or done anything to express hostility to 'Salvadoran females' in general, as opposed to having made statements and taken actions based upon their personal feelings about the respondent, their daughter." *Matter of A-C-A-A-*, 28 I. & N. Dec. 1984, 93 (A.G., 2020).

21. *Matter of A-C-A-A-*, 28 I. & N. Dec. 84, 94; and n5 (A.G., 2020).

22. See the discussion of *Matter of A-C-A-A* in chapter 5.

23. *Matter of A-B-*, 28 I. & N. Dec. 199 (A.G., 2021).

24. See, e.g., *Crespin-Vallidares v. Holder*, 632 F. 3rd 117, 125 (4th Cir., 2011).

25. *Matter of L-E-A-*, 27 I. & N. Dec. 581, 582 (A.G., 2019). On December 10, 2020, the Ninth Circuit vacated *Matter of E-R-A-L-*, 27 I. & N. Dec. 767 (BIA 2020), in which the BIA had rejected the family and landowner-based particular social groups presented by a Guatemalan asylum seeker who was targeted by a drug cartel because his family owned a farm in Guatemala. *Albizures-Lopez v. Barr,* No. 20-70640, 2020 WL 7406164, 2020 U.S. App. LEXIS 38725 (9th Cir. Dec. 10, 2020).

26. *SAP v. Barr*, Case 1:2019-cv-03549, D.D.C. (filed Nov. 22, 2019).

27. The procedure for adjudicating affirmative applications is discussed in chapter 1.

28. The asylum clinic at Georgetown Law that two of the authors direct has represented many journalists and political dissidents who were threatened with death, obtained tourist or student visas to come to the United States, and applied for asylum after their arrival. Some of them initially hoped to return home but sought asylum only when their permitted stay in the United States was drawing to a close and they realized that they faced renewed persecution if they returned.

29. American Immigration Lawyers' Association, *AILA Policy Brief: USCIS's "No Blank Space" Policy Leads to Capricious Rejections of Benefits Requests* (Oct. 22, 2020), https://perma.cc/4EHJ -GF3M.

30. National Immigration Litigation Alliance, Northwest Immigrant

Rights Project, and Van Der Hout, LLP, *USCIS Updates Intake Policies and Halts Application of the Rejection Policy in Response to Vangala v. USCIS: Frequently Asked Questions* (Jan. 14, 2021), https://immigrationlitigation.org/wp-content/uploads/2021/01/Vangala-FAQ-and-Updated-USCIS-Guidance.pdf. See also Charles Davis, *Bureaucracy as a Weapon: How the Trump Administration Is Slowing Asylum Cases, Guardian* (Dec. 23, 2019), www.theguardian.com/us-news/2019/dec/23/us-immigration-trump-asylum-seekers; Catherine Rampell, *The Trump Administration's No-Blanks Policy Is the Latest Kafkaesque Plan Designed to Curb Immigration, Washington Post* (Aug. 6, 2020).

31. *Vangala, et al. v. US Citizenship and Immigration Services, et al.,* Class Action Complaint for Injunctive and Declaratory Relief, Case 3:20-cv-08143 (N.D.C.A. filed Nov. 19, 2020).

32. Proposed Form I-589.

33. See Comment of National Immigrant Justice Center (Aug. 14, 2020), on file with the authors.

34. The operation and origin of this rule are discussed at the end of chapter 1.

35. Department of Homeland Security, *Asylum Application, Interview, and Employment Authorization for Applicants,* 85 *Fed. Reg.* 38532 (June 26, 2020); 8 *C.F.R.* part 208, 247a. If an asylum officer or immigration judge denies the asylum claim within that 365-day waiting period, the applicant is not eligible for a work permit even if the case is on appeal.

36. Any delay by an applicant not resolved by time of filing for a work permit will result in its denial. Id.

37. Angela Brauer, *Immigration Court Confirms Years-Long Backlog of Cases,* CBS, June 4, 2020, https://perma.cc/9JYT-M2NB.

38. *Casa de Maryland, et al. v. Wolf,* case 8:20-cv-2118 (filed July 21, 2020); *Asylumworks, et al. v. Wolf,* case 1:20-cv-03815 (filed Dec. 22, 2020) https://immigrantjustice.org/sites/default/files/content-type/press-release/documents/2020-12/Complaint_AsylumWorks-v-Wolf.PDF. The plaintiff organizations won the first skirmish in the *Casa de Maryland* litigation, obtaining a court order that barred DHS from withholding employment authorization from their members under the terms of the new reg

ulation. But the court declined to apply its ruling on a nationwide basis. *Memorandum Opinion in Casa de Maryland v. Wolf* (Sept. 11, 2020), https://perma.cc/ZGU2-359N.

39. USCIS, *Policy Manual, Chapter 5: Discretion—Section A: Discretionary Authority and Applicability*, www.uscis.gov/policy-man ual/volume-10-part-a-chapter-5.

40. *Presidential Memorandum on Additional Mechanisms to Enhance Border Security and Restore Integrity to Our Immigration System*, at Sec. 3(c) (Apr. 29, 2019).

41. The final rule can be found here: Department of Homeland Security, *US Citizenship and Immigration Services Fee Schedule and Changes to Certain Other Immigration Benefit Request Requirements*, 85 Fed. Reg. 46788 (Aug. 3, 2020). The rule exempts unaccompanied minors from the $50 fee.

42. *Immigrant Legal Resource Center, et al. v. Wolf,* case 4:20-cv-05883-JSW, *Order Granting Plaintiffs' Motion for Preliminary Injunction and Request for Stay of Effective Date of Rule and Denying Request for Administrative Stay* (filed Sept. 29, 2020) (enjoining the rule based on violations of the Homeland Security Act in conjunction with the Federal Vacancies Reform Act, because acting Secretary of the United States Department of Homeland Security Chad Wolf and Senior Official Performing the Duties of Deputy Secretary of Homeland Security Kenneth T. Cuccinelli were unlawfully appointed to those roles, as well as the Administrative Procedures Act). On December 28, 2020, the government voluntarily dismissed its appeal, which means that the fee rule remains enjoined.

43. 8 U.S.C. Sec. 1229(a)(1).

44. 8 U.S.C. Sec. 1229a(b)(4)(A).

45. 8 U.S.C. Sec. 1229a(b)(4)(B).

46. Id.

47. 8 U.S.C. Sec. 1229(c)(1)(A).

48. 8 C.F.R. Sec. 1003; 8 U.S.C. Sec. 1252(d).

49. White House, *Remarks by President Trump Before Marine One Departure*, May 30, 2019, https://perma.cc/TS8G-H25Y.

50. TRAC Immigration, *Backlog of Pending Cases in Immigration Courts as of March 2020* (May 26, 2020).

51. White House, *Remarks by President Trump and NATO Secretary General Jens Stoltenberg Before Bilateral Meeting* (Apr. 2, 2019), https://perma.cc/5ZKY-P53D.

52. Donald J. Trump (@realDonaldTrump), Twitter (June 24, 2018, 8:02AMEST), https://twitter.com/realdonaldtrump/status/1010900865602019329?lang=en.

53. The possible threat of demotion or transfer was not lost on judges who could recall or were told about the 2002 purge of the less enforcement-oriented members of the Board of Immigration Appeals, which is discussed in chapter 2.

54. Executive Office for Immigration Review, *EOIR Performance Plan [for] Adjudicative Employees*, https://perma.cc/FT7G-SVNH.

55. *Memorandum from James McHenry, Director of the Executive Office for Immigration Review, to All Judges*, provided to Michelle Mendez, Catholic Legal Immigration Network, on July 24, 2018, in response to Freedom of Information Act request, https://perma.cc/FT5B-L6ZD. For a photograph of the dashboard, see Beth Fertig, *Presiding Under Pressure*, WNYC (May 21, 2019), https://perma.cc/MAB4-KWWR.

56. The association is the public employees union to which the judges belong. As noted later in this chapter, the Trump administration initiated proceedings to decertify the union.

57. Liz Robbins, *In Immigration Courts, It Is Judges vs. Justice Department*, New York Times (Sept. 7, 2018). The metrics were challenged by several individual immigrants and immigrant advocacy organizations in *Las Americas Immigrant Advocacy Center v. Trump*, case 3:19-cv-2051 (D. Ore., Dec. 18, 2019). The plaintiffs assert that by tying career advancement to speedy adjudication, the metrics give judges a financial interest in the outcomes of their cases. As of this writing, no decision on the legality of the metrics has been rendered, but in July 2020, a federal judge rejected the government's motion to dismiss the case.

58. Stephen Franklin, *The Revolt of the Judges*, American Prospect (June 23, 2020). For a more detailed explanation of how the metrics detract from due process for respondents facing removal, see Mimi Tsankov, *Judicial Independence Sidelined: Just One More Symptom of an Immigration Court System Reeling*, 56 Cal. W. L.

Rev. 35 (2019). The association's video is at https://youtu.be
/wfZtqHtNyTY.

59. For years, immigration courts had "administratively closed" or
"terminated" cases without reaching their merits, sometimes at
the request of the government and sometimes at the request of
the immigrant, when there was little point in keeping it on the
docket. For example, if the judge has some reason to believe that
the immigrant would receive a visa in the near future and DHS
would allow the individual to immigrate, the judge might see no
reason to hear the case and might postpone or end it while still
allowing DHS to reinstitute it if, for some reason, the immigrant
did not get the visa. In two rulings, Attorney General Sessions
decreed that the immigration judges lacked the power to "administratively close" or to "terminate" cases except in very narrow
circumstances. *Matter of Castro-Tum*, 27 I. & N. Dec. 271 (A.G.,
2018); *Matter of S-O-G & F-D-P-*, 27 I. & N. Dec. 462 (A.G., 2018).
Two federal courts of appeals, however, held that contrary to Sessions's ruling in *Castro-Tum*, judges do have the general authority to
administratively close cases. *Zuniga Romero v. Barr*, 937 F. 3rd 282
(4th Cir., 2019); *Morales v. Barr*, 973 F. 3rd 656 (7th Cir., 2020).

60. For decades, immigration courts had granted continuances in
pending cases to allow the immigrant to pursue administrative
avenues, other than asylum, for being permitted to remain in the
United States. For example, an applicant for asylum might also be
a victim of trafficking and might have a chance to receive a "T"
visa on that basis if the case were continued. Attorney General
Sessions limited the authority of immigration judges to continue
cases to allow immigrants to seek relief from DHS, suggesting
that in the interest of efficiency, fewer continuances should be
granted. His decision directs immigration judges to require an
immigrant who seeks a continuance to provide written evidence
showing that administrative relief is likely, and the immigration
judge must provide a reasoned explanation if a continuance is
granted. *Matter of L-A-B-R-*, 27 I. & N. Dec. 405 (A.G., 2018).

61. For examples of how oral statements in court can make a critical
difference, enabling a migrant to win asylum, see Jeffrey S. Chase,
Just One More Thing (blog, May 27, 2020), https://perma.cc

/JT3S-DCFX. See, e.g., *Hernandez-Chacon v. Barr*, 948 F. 3rd 94 (2nd Cir., 2020), where the immigrant's oral statement in court that she told her persecutor that she had "every right" to flee from his attempted rape was critical to her claim that she was threatened with persecution on account of her political opinion.

62. *Matter of E-F-H-L-*, 26 I. & N. Dec. 319 (BIA, 2014), citing 8 C.F.R. Sec. 1240.11(c)(3)(iii).

63. In 2016, fewer than 40 percent of immigrants had lawyers in immigration court. National Immigrant Justice Center, Access to Counsel (undated, but reporting data from 2016).

64. *Matter of E-F-H-L-*, 27 I. & N. Dec. 226 (A.G., 2018).

65. See, e.g., Jeffrey S. Chase, *The AG's Strange Decision in Matter of E-F-H-L* (blog, Mar. 10, 2018). Chase is a former immigration judge.

66. Jaya Ramji-Nogales, Andrew I. Schoenholtz, and Philip G. Schrag, *Refugee Roulette: Disparities in Asylum Adjudication*, 60 *Stan. L. Rev.* 295, 347 (2007): Judges with no work experience as law enforcers granted asylum 48 percent of the time, while those with one to ten years of such experience had an average grant rate of 40 to 43 percent, and those with more than ten years of enforcement experience had an average grant rate of only 31 percent.

67. Priscilla Alvarez, *Jeff Sessions Is Quietly Transforming the Nation's Immigration Courts*, Atlantic (Oct. 17, 2018), https://perma.cc /SP5U-7T9C.

68. Id.

69. Noah Lanard, *The Trump Administration's Court-Packing Scheme Fills Immigration Appeals Board with Hardliners*, Mother Jones (Aug. 29, 2019).

70. Id.

71. Tanvi Misra, *DOJ Changed Hiring to Promote Restrictive Immigration Judges*, Roll Call (Oct. 29, 2019), https://perma.cc/W83C -TMPJ. For a follow-up story, based on documents obtained through the Freedom of Information Act, see Tanvi Misra, *DOJ Hiring Changes May Help Trump's Plan to Curb Immigration*, Roll Call (May 4, 2020), https://perma.cc/V6VR-4YC4.

72. Lanard, *Trump Administration's Court-Packing Scheme*.

73. Misra, *DOJ Changed Hiring.*

74. Richard Gonzales, *Trump Administration Seeks Decertification of Immigration Judges' Union,* NPR (Aug. 12, 2019), https://perma.cc/293Y-SZQ2.

75. Eric Katz, *Trump Administration Makes Its Case to Break Up Immigration Judges' Union* (Jan. 7, 2020).

76. *Dept. of Justice v. National Association of Immigration Judges,* 71 FLRA No. 207 (Nov. 2, 2020), https://perma.cc/4PSA-K2N8.

77. *Dept. of Justice v. National Association of Immigration Judges.*

78. Erich Wagner, *FLRA Overturns Its Own Regional Director, Busts Immigration Judges' Union, Government Executive* (Nov. 3, 2020).

79. *National Association of Immigration Judges v. McHenry,* case 1:20-cv-00731 (E.D. Va), Complaint (filed July 1, 2020), https://knightcolumbia.org/documents/3c53028907/2020.07.01_ECF-1_Complaint.pdf.

80. *Nat'l Assn. of Immig. Judges v. McHenry,* case 20-01868 (4th Cir.).

81. American Bar Association, *Adult Legal Orientation Program for Immigrant Detainees (LOP)* (undated; last visited May 28, 2020).

82. See, e.g., Capital Area Immigrants' Rights Coalition, *Detained Adult Program* (undated; last visited May 28, 2020).

83. Vanessa Romo, *Justice Department Will Pause a Legal Advice Program for Detained Immigrants,* NPR (Apr. 12, 2018), https://perma.cc/C8BN-MU7W.

84. Executive Office for Immigration Review, *Cost Savings Analysis: The EOIR Legal Orientation Program* (Apr. 4, 2012), https://perma.cc/JKJ5-D7WM.

85. *Sessions Resumes Free Legal Assistance Program for Detained Immigrants—for Now,* CNN (Apr. 25, 2018), https://perma.cc/3PKL-3YNX.

86. TRAC, *EOIR's Data Release on Asylum So Deficient Public Should Not Rely on Accuracy of Court Records* (June 3, 2020). For a critique by a former immigration judge of EOIR's statistics during the Trump administration, see Jeffrey S. Chase, *EOIR's New Math,* Dec. 12, 2020, https://perma.cc/8CKM-6EX8.

87. See Catholic Legal Immigration Network, *Department of State Shifts Human Rights Practices Honduras Comparison Chart 1* (Oct. 20, 2020), https://cliniclegal.org/resources/asylum-and

-refugee-law/clinic-department-state-shifts-human-rights-re
ports-comparison.

88. Asylum Research Centre, *Comparative Analysis: U.S. Department
    of State's Country Reports on Human Rights Practices 2016–2019*
    (2020), https://perma.cc/6NU2-X59P.

89. Department of Homeland Security, Office of Inspector General,
    *In the Matter of Murphy, Brian, Principal Deputy Under Secretary,
    Department of Homeland Security, Office of Intelligence & Analysis,*
    Whistleblower Reprisal Complaint, at 9 (Sept. 8, 2020), https://
    intelligence.house.gov/uploadedfiles/murphy_wb_dhs_oig
    _complaint9.8.20.pdf.

90. TRAC Immigration, *Asylum Denial Rates Continue to Climb* (Oct.
    28, 2020), https://trac.syr.edu/immigration/reports/630/.

Chapter 4

1. 8 U.S.C. 1158. This conforms to Article 31 of the Refugee Convention, which specifically states that contracting states shall
   not impose penalties on refugees in connection with illegal
   entry or presence. Convention relating to the Status of Refugees (1951), https://www.ohchr.org/en/professionalinterest
   /pages/statusofrefugees.aspx.

2. Julia Ainsley, *Stephen Miller Wants Border Patrol, Not Asylum Officers, to Determine Migrant Asylum Claims*, NBC News (July 29,
   2019), https://perma.cc/N9GM-6MUW.

3. Historically, immigration judges have varied greatly in their re-
   ceptivity to asylum claims. Some judges in large urban immigration courts, where they are assigned randomly to cases, have had
   percentage rates of granting asylum in the low single digits, while
   others in the same court have had rates well above 70 percent. Jaya
   Ramji-Nogales, Andrew I. Schoenholtz, and Philip G. Schrag, *Refugee Roulette: Disparities in Asylum Adjudication*, 60 *Stan. L. Rev.*
   295, 335–49 (2007). These disparities have persisted. In fiscal
   year 2020, immigration judges in New York had grant rates from
   5 percent to 97 percent, depending on the judge. TRAC Immigration, *Asylum Denial Rates Continue to Climb* (Oct. 28, 2020),
   https://trac.syr.edu/immigration/reports/630/.

4. The House bill that eventually became the Illegal Immigration Reform and Immigrant Responsibility Act of 1996 (IIRIRA) prescribed that a migrant could pass the credible fear screening test only by showing that "it is more probable than not" that he or she is telling the truth and that there was a significant possibility that an immigration judge could find that the applicant qualified for asylum under the law. As Senator Orrin Hatch, the floor manager of the bill, described the conference committee report, it "struck a compromise by rejecting the [House's] higher standard of credibility. The standard adopted in the conference report is intended to be a *low screening standard* for admission into the usual full asylum process." Statement of Sen. Hatch, 142 *Cong. Rec.* S11,491 (1996) (emphasis added).

5. Dept. of Homeland Security, *Credible Fear Cases Completed and Referrals for Credible Fear Interview* [FY 2007–18] (last visited May 21, 2020).

6. Id.

7. The Obama administration had also sought to change the wording, but in less drastic ways. The 2006 lesson plan had quoted Senator Hatch's language to the effect that the credible fear test was a "low screening standard," but when border apprehensions rose in 2014, as discussed in chapter 2, the Obama administration deleted that explanation from the lesson plan. Catholic Legal Immigration Network, Inc. (CLINIC), *Credible Fear Lesson Plans Comparison Chart: 2006 → 2014 → 2017 → 2019* (Oct. 4, 2019) (last visited May 21, 2020).

8. The Trump administration deleted earlier versions of the asylum lesson plans from government websites, making it very difficult for historians and other academics to track the changes that it made in the credible fear and other asylum lesson plans. See Chantal da Silva, *USCIS Deleted Hundreds of Web Pages on U.S. Asylum Protocol After Trump Took Office, Watchdog Says, Newsweek* (May 31, 2018), https://perma.cc/Q884-8YPG. The administration's justification was that the deleted lesson plans were "outdated and no longer being used." Id.

9. See U.S. Citizenship and Immigration Services (USCIS), *Les-*

son Plan Overview (Apr. 30, 2019); and CLINIC, *Credible Fear Lesson Plans Comparison Chart.*

10. USCIS, *Lesson Plan Overview: Credible Fear of Persecution and Torture Determinations* (Feb. 13, 2017).

11. See USCIS, *Lesson Plan Overview* (Apr. 30, 2019).

12. Id. The Trump guidance also changed the lesson plan in several other ways less favorable to applicants. See CLINIC, *Credible Fear Lesson Plans Comparison Chart.*

13. *Memorandum Opinion in Kiakombua v. Wolf,* Case 1:19-cv-01872 (D.D.C., 2020), https://perma.cc/UF4A-CWHC; *Kiakombua v. Wolf,* 20-5372 (D.C. Cir., filed Dec. 17, 2020) (appeal).

14. The Senate's floor manager for IIRIRA, which authorized expedited removal, stated on the floor that "screening would be done by fully trained asylum officers supervised by officers who have not only had comparable training but have also had substantial experience adjudicating asylum applications. This should prevent the potential that was in [a prior] bill provisions for erroneous decisions by lower level immigration officials at points of entry. I feel very strongly that the appropriate, fully trained asylum officers conduct the screening in the summary exclusion process." 142 *Cong. Rec.* S11492 (daily ed., Sept. 27, 1996).

15. U.S. Government Accountability Office, *Immigration: Actions Needed to Strengthen USCIS's Oversight and Data Quality of Credible and Reasonable Fear Screenings,* 26–27 (Feb. 2020).

16. Camilo Montoya-Galvez, CBS News, *Border Patrol Agents Now Screening Migrants for "Credible Fear" Under Controversial Pilot Program* (Sept. 20, 2019), https://perma.cc/DRV9-LMZE; U.S. Government Accountability Office, *Immigration,* 11 n. f.

17. Molly O'Toole, *Border Patrol Agents, Rather Than Asylum Officers, Interviewing Families for "Credible Fear," Los Angeles Times* (Sept. 19, 2019), www.latimes.com/politics/story/2019-09-19/border-patrol-interview-migrant-families-credible-fear.

18. Hamed Aleaziz, *Under Trump's New Project, Border Patrol Agents Have Approved Fewer Than Half of Asylum Screenings,* Buzzfeed News (Nov. 7, 2019).

19. U.S. Government Accountability Office, *Immigration*.

20. Id. See Hamed Aleaziz.

21. USCIS, *Semi-Monthly Credible Fear and Reasonable Fear Receipts and Decisions by Outcome Type: June 1, 2019 to June 15, 2020*.

22. See Aleaziz.

23. Preliminary injunction in *A. B.–B. v. Morgan, Case 20-cv-846* (D.D.C., Aug. 31, 2020).

24. By the time the decision was rendered, the Trump administration had barred nearly all migrants arriving from Mexico and was no longer routinely conducting credible fear interviews at the southern border. See the discussion below of the closing of the border that the Trump administration claimed was justified by the COVID-19 pandemic.

25. The Department of Homeland Security's Office of Inspector General found that, through its metering policies (discussed further infra), CBP pushed asylum seekers to enter without inspection. Once they had done so, the parents could be prosecuted for unlawful entry, which the Trump administration used to justify separating them from their children. See https://www.oig.dhs.gov/sites/default/files/assets/2018-10/OIG-18-84-Sep18.pdf.

26. Ingrid Eagly and Steven Shafer, *Measuring In Absentia Removal in Immigration Court, Univ. of Penn. L. Rev.* 168 (2020); Ingrid Eagly, Steven Shafer, and Jana Whalley, *Detaining Families: A Study of Asylum Adjudication in Family Detention, California Law Review* 106 (2018): 847–48, figure 15.

27. ICE, *Family Case Management Program (FMCP) Closeout Report*, at 7 (Feb. 2018); Congressional Research Service, *Immigration: Alternatives to Detention Programs* 10–14 (July 8, 2019), https://perma.cc/QTP2-UV3C.

28. $319 is the figure reported by Department of Homeland Security, *Congressional Budget Justification FY 2018, U.S. Immigration and Customs Enforcement*, II: 50 (2017).

29. Caitlin Dickerson, *Trump Administration Targets Parents in New Immigration Crackdown, New York Times* (July 1, 2017). Even though they had entered the United States with at least one

parent, after CBP separated these children from their parent(s), CBP processed the children as unaccompanied minors and placed them in ORR custody.

30. See Philip G. Schrag, *Baby Jails: The Fight to End the Incarceration of Migrant Children in America 217–18* (2020).

31. Majority Staff Report, Committee on the Judiciary, House of Representatives, *The Trump Administration's Family Separation Policy: Trauma, Destruction, and Chaos*, at 6 (Oct. 2020), https://perma.cc/G5ND-ZCWB; U.S. Government Accountability Office, *Unaccompanied Children: Agency Efforts to Reunify Children Separated from Parents at the Border*, at 14 (Oct. 2018), https://perma.cc/9NDJ-JCUL.

32. Attorney General Jefferson B. Sessions, *Memorandum for All Federal Prosecutors on Renewed Commitment to Criminal Immigration Enforcement*, U.S. Department of Justice (Apr. 11, 2017), https://perma.cc/Q6JE-P4CU.

33. Majority Staff Report, Committee on the Judiciary, House of Representatives, *The Trump Administration's Family Separation Policy: Trauma, Destruction, and Chaos*, at 7 (Oct. 2020), https://perma.cc/G5ND-ZCWB.

34. Department of Homeland Security, Office of Inspector General, *DHS Lacked Technology Needed to Successfully Account for Separated Migrant Families* (Nov. 2019), https://perma.cc/6Z TK-8LGC.

35. *Policy Options to Respond to Border Surge of Illegal Immigration* (Dec. 2017) (unpublished memorandum from the Department of Homeland Security), https://perma.cc/A3HB-TL84; Senator Jeff Merkley, *Press Release: In Bombshell NBC News Story, Merkley Reveals Secret Trump Administration Plan to Create Border Crisis* (Jan. 17, 2019), https://perma.cc/L5RY-C87H; Philip Bump, *Here Are the Administration Officials Who Have Said That Family Separation Is Meant as a Deterrent, Washington Post* (June 19, 2018), www.washingtonpost.com/news/politics /wp/2018/06/19/here-are-the-administration-officials-who -have-said-that-family-separation-is-meant-as-a-deterrent/.

36. Amended complaint, *Ms. L. v. ICE*, Case 18-cv-00428-DMS-

MDD (S.D. Calif., Mar. 9, 2018); Derek Hawkins, *A Mother and Child Fled Congo Fearing Death. ICE Has Held Them Separately for Months, Lawsuit Says, Washington Post* (Feb. 27, 2018); *Ms. L. v. U.S. Immigration & Customs Enf't ("ICE")*, 310 F. Supp. 3rd 1133 (S.D. Cal., 2018).

37. Attorney General Jefferson B. Sessions, *Memorandum for Federal Prosecutors Along the Southwest Border on Zero-Tolerance for Offenses Under 8 U.S.C. § 1325(a)* (Apr. 6, 2018), https://perma.cc/BW5F-2QYM.

38. Michael D. Shear, Katie Benner, and Michael S. Schmidt, *"We Need to Take Away Children," No Matter How Young, Justice Dep. Officials Said, New York Times* (Oct. 6, 2020), https://perma.cc/FL9Z-ENAU.

39. *R. I. L-R- v. Johnson*, 80 F. 3rd 164 (D.D.C. 2015). A preliminary injunction against using the deterrence justification was dissolved without prejudice to reinstatement when ICE agreed not to base its policies on a deterrence rationale. Order in *R.I. L-R- v. Johnson* (June 29, 2015). The Trump administration apparently did not feel bound by the Obama administration's agreement.

40. National Public Radio, *Transcript: White House Chief of Staff John Kelly's Interview with NPR* (May 11, 2018), https://perma.cc/U5PH-4PU4.

41. Ginger Thompson, *Listen to Children Who've Just Been Separated from Their Parents at the Border*, Pro Publica (June 18, 2018), https://perma.cc/SN5F-YC2X.

42. *Ms. L. v. U.S. Immigration & Customs Enf't ("ICE")*, 310 F. Supp. 3rd 1133 (S.D. Cal., 2018).

43. Office of the Inspector General, U.S. Department of Homeland Security, *Special Review: Initial Observations Regarding Family Separation Issues Under the Zero Tolerance Policy* (Sept. 27, 2018), https://www.oig.dhs.gov/sites/default/files/assets/2018-10/OIG-18-84-Sep18.pdf.

44. Richard Gonzalez, *New Report: U.S. Lacked Technology to Account for Separated Families*, NPR (Nov. 27, 2019), https://www.npr.org/2019/11/27/783513721/new-report-says-u-s-lacked-technology-to-account-for-separated-families.

45. Jacob Soboroff and Julia Ainsley, *Lawyers Can't Find the Parents of 666 Migrant Kids, a Higher Number Than Previously Reported*, NBC News (Nov. 9, 2020).

46. Order granting plaintiffs' motion for classwide preliminary injunction in *Ms. L. v. ICE* (June 26, 2018); Department of Justice, Office of the Inspector General, *Review of the Department of Justice's Planning and Implementation of Its Zero Tolerance Policy and Its Coordination with the Departments of Homeland Security and Health and Human Services* (Jan. 2021), https://oig.justice.gov/sites/default/files/reports/21-028_0.pdf.

47. "The government readily keeps track of personal property of detainees in criminal and immigration proceedings. Money, important documents, and automobiles, to name a few, are routinely catalogued, stored, tracked and produced upon a detainee's release, at all levels—state and federal, citizen and alien. Yet, the government has no system in place to keep track of, provide effective communication with, and promptly produce alien children. The unfortunate reality is that under the present system migrant children are not accounted for with the same efficiency and accuracy as property. Certainly, that cannot satisfy the requirements of due process." *Ms. L. v. U.S. Immigration & Customs Enf't ("ICE")*, 310 F. Supp. 3rd 1133, 1144 (S.D. Cal., 2018). See also Jonathan Blitzer, *A New Report Shows the Depths of Trump's Negligence, New Yorker* (Dec. 6, 2019), www.newyorker.com/news/news-desk/a-new-report-on-family-separations-shows-the-depths-of-trumps-negligence; see also U.S. Government Accountability Office, GAO-19-163, *Unaccompanied Children: Agency Efforts to Reunify Children Separated from Parents at the Border* (2018); U.S. Department of Homeland Security, Office of the Inspector General, OIG-18-84, *Special Review: Initial Observations Regarding Family Separation Issues Under the Zero Tolerance Policy 9* (Sept. 27, 2018).

48. *Flores v. Johnson*, 212 F. Supp. 3rd 864 (C.D. Calif., 2015).

49. *Flores v. Lynch*, 828 F. 3rd 898 (9th Cir., 2016). The Ninth Circuit determined, however, that the Flores agreement conferred no rights on the parents, paving the way for family separation.

50. *Defendant's Memorandum of Points and Authorities in Support of*

Ex Parte Application for Relief from the Flores Settlement Agreement, Flores v. Sessions, 2018 U.S. Dist. Lexis 115488, CV 85-4544-DMG (C.D. Cal., June 21, 2018).

51. *Flores v. Sessions*, No. CV 85-4544-DMG (AGRx), 2018 U.S. Dist. Lexis 115488 (C.D. Cal., July 9, 2018).

52. ICE et al., *Apprehension, Processing, Care, and Custody of Alien Minors and Unaccompanied Alien Children*, 83 Fed. Reg. 45486 (proposed Sept. 7, 2018) (to be codified at 45 C.F.R. pt. 410).

53. *Matter of M-S-, 27 I, & N. Dec. 509* (Attorney General 2019), *Overruling Matter of X-K-, 23 I. & N. Dec. 731* (2005).

54. *Padilla v. ICE*, 953 F. 3rd 1134 (9th Cir. 2020).

55. *ICE v. Padilla*, ___ U.S. ___, 2021 U.S. LEXIS 315 (2021).

56. R. J. Vogt, *Immigrant Bond Grants Stagnate Despite More Counsel, Law 360* (June 28, 2020), www.law360.com/immigration/articles/1287209/immigrant-bond-grants-stagnate-despite-more-counsel.

57. ICE et al., *Apprehension, Processing, Care, and Custody of Alien Minors and Unaccompanied Alien Children*, 84 Fed. Reg. 44392 (Aug. 23, 2019).

58. Priscilla Alvarez, *California and 19 Other States Sue Over Rule Allowing Prolonged Detention of Migrant Families*, CNN (Aug. 26, 2019), www.cnn.com/2019/08/26/politics/states-sue-flores-settlement-agreement-challenge-trump-rule/index.html.

59. *Flores v. Barr*, 407 F. Supp. 3d 909 (C. D. Cal., 2019); *Flores v. Rosen*, ___ F. 3d ___; 2020 U.S. App. LEXIS 40573 (9th Cir. 2020).

60. *Matter of M. A. C. O, 27 I. & N. Dec. 477* (BIA, 2018).

61. For a more extended discussion of the history of detention of migrant children before and during the Trump administration, see Philip G. Schrag, *Baby Jails: The Fight to End the Incarceration of Refugee Children in America* (2020).

62. Findings of Fact and Conclusions of Law in *Ramirez v. Immigration* and Customs Enforcement, Case 18-cv-00508 (D.D.C., July 2, 2020); Spencer Hsu, *ICE Unlawfully Jails Unaccompanied Migrant Children Once They Turn 18, Judge Rules, Washington Post* (July 2, 2020).

63. Maria Woltjen, *The White House Is Quietly Deporting Children*, New York Times (June 22, 2020), https://www.nytimes.com/2020/06/22/opinion/coronavirus-children-border-deportation.html?searchResultPosition=1; Molly O'Toole and Cindy Carcamo, *New Rulings Amid Coronavirus Could Force Trump to Release Migrant Children and Parents*, Los Angeles Times (Mar. 31, 2020), www.latimes.com/politics/story/2020-03-31/trump-ruling-release-migrant-children-parents-coronavirus.

64. Nick Miroff, *Migrant Parents Could Face Fateful Choice: Be Separated from Their Children or Stay Together in Jail*, Washington Post (Oct. 23, 2020).

65. The practice of informal pushbacks began as early as the summer of 2016, under the Obama administration.

66. Human Rights First, *Crossing the Line: U.S. Border Agents Illegally Reject Asylum Seekers*, at 5–7 (May 2017), www.humanrightsfirst.org/sites/default/files/hrf-crossing-the-line-report.pdf; See *Second Amended Complaint for Declaratory and Injunctive Relief*, in *Al Otro Lado v. McAleenan*, Case 3:17-cv-02366 (S. D. Calif., Nov. 13, 2018), https://perma.cc/9CYM-CLFV.

67. Human Rights First, *Crossing the Line*, 11-14; Second Amended Complaint in *Al Otro Lado v. McAleenan*, at 1, 9, 10, 46, 50, 53, 57, 58, 61 and 62.

68. Human Rights First, *Crossing the Line*, 5–6.

69. DHS Office of Inspector General, *CBP Has Taken Steps to Limit Processing of Undocumented Aliens at Ports of Entry*, at 10–16 (Oct. 27, 2020), https://www.oig.dhs.gov/sites/default/files/assets/2020-10/OIG-21-02-Oct20.pdf.

70. CBP had briefly implemented metering at the San Ysidro port during an emergency situation under the Obama administration in 2016. James Fredrick, *"Metering" at the Border*, NPR (June 29, 2019), www.npr.org/2019/06/29/737268856/metering-at-the-border.

71. See *Special Review: Initial Observations Regarding Family Separation Issues Under the Zero Tolerance*, DHS Office of the Inspector General, at 5-7 (Sept. 27, 2018) (hereafter, *OIG Metering Report*); Fredrick, 2019.

72. Office of the Inspector General, U.S. Department of Homeland

Security, *Investigation of Alleged Violations of Immigration Laws at the Tecate, California, Port of Entry by U.S. Customs and Border Protection Personnel*, at 2 (Sept. 26, 2019).

73. *Al Otro Lado v. McAleenan*, 394 F. Supp. 3rd 1168 (S.D. Calif., 2019).

74. *Order Granting Motion for Class Certification*, in *Al Otro Lado v. Wolf*, Case 17-cv-02366 (S.D. Calif., Aug. 6, 2020).

75. *Order Clarifying Preliminary Injunction*, in *Al Otro Lado v. Wolf*, 3:17-cv-02366 (S.D. Calif., Oct. 30, 2020).

76. Strauss Center, *Metering Update: November 2019*, www.strauscenter.org/publications/metering-update-2/.

77. Strauss Center, *Metering Update: February 2020*, 1, www.strausscenter.org/wp-content/uploads/MeteringUpdate_February_2020.pdf.

78. Strauss Center, *Metering Update: May 2020*, 2, www.strausscenter.org/wp-content/uploads/MeteringUpdate_200528.pdf.

79. Id., 1.

80. See the section on the Migrant Protection Protocols, text, at n. 89, infra.

81. More than a half million asylum seekers arrived during fiscal year 2018, about a 25 percent increase over fiscal year 2017. See Office of Immigration Statistics, U.S. Department of Homeland Security, *2018 Yearbook of Immigration Statistics 95–97*, www.dhs.gov/sites/default/files/publications/immigration-statistics/yearbook/2018/yearbook_immigration_statistics_2018.pdf.

82. IIRIRA, *Div. C of Pub. L. 104–208, 110 Stat. 3009-546*, enacted Sept. 30, 1996, now 8 U.S.C. 1158(a)(1) (INA 208(a)(1)) (emphasis added).

83. Deptartments of Homeland Security and Justice, *Aliens Subject to a Bar on Entry Under Certain Presidential Proclamations*, 83 *Fed. Reg. 55934* (Nov. 8, 2018) (interim final rule).

84. See www.whitehouse.gov/presidential-actions/presidential-proclamation-addressing-mass-migration-southern-border-united-states/.

85. *East Bay Sanctuary Covenant v. Trump* (EBSC I), 349 F. Supp. 3rd 838 (N.D. Cal., 2018).

86. *East Bay Sanctuary Covenant v. Trump* (EBSC II), 932 F. 3rd 742 (9th Cir., 2018).

87. *East Bay Sanctuary Covenant v. Trump* (EBSC III), 354 F. Supp. 3rd 1094 (N.D. Cal., 2018).

88. *Trump v. East Bay Sanctuary Covenant*, 139 U.S. 782 (2018).

89. *East Bay Sanctuary Covenant v. Trump*, 950 F. 3rd 1242 (9th Cir., 2020), http://cdn.ca9.uscourts.gov/datastore/general/2020 /02/28/18-17436_opinion.pdf.

90. *EBSC II,* 932 F. 3rd at 774. Appointed by President George W. Bush to the Ninth Circuit, Judge Bybee previously served in the Bush administration's Office of Legal Counsel at the Justice Department. A D.C. District Court decision vacating the interim final rule is on appeal. *O.A. v. Trump,* Civ. No. 18-2718 (D.D.C. 2019).

91. U.S. Department of Homeland Security, *Secretary Kirstjen M. Nielsen Announces Historic Action to Confront Illegal Immigration* (Dec. 12, 2018), press release, https://perma.cc/3EAS-TDVX; see www.dhs.gov/news/2019/01/24/migrant-protection-pro tocols; *Assessment of Migrant Protection Protocols (MPP)*, U.S. Department of Homeland Security, at 3 (Oct. 28, 2019) (hereafter *MPP Assessment*). Mexican nationals and unaccompanied children are supposedly exempt from MPP, but the Department of Homeland Security has sometimes not honored the exception. Several unaccompanied minors, generally those with children of their own, have been returned to Mexico, sometimes even when their age was known to the Department of Homeland Security. HRF 2019, at 9–10. This policy results in the separation of children from their parents or siblings. HRF 2019, at 8–9.

92. See the discussion, infra n. 122, of the reasons why Congress enacted 8 U.S.C. § 1225(b)(2)(C), responding to the decision in *Matter of Sanchez-Avila*, 21 I. & N. Dec. 444 (BIA, 1996).

93. Human Rights First, *A Year of Horrors: The Trump Administration's Illegal Returns of Asylum Seekers to Danger in Mexico*, 3 (Jan. 2020), www.humanrightsfirst.org/sites/default/files /AYearofHorrors-MPP.pdf. The number of new individuals forced to wait in Mexico fell after the Trump administration

began using even more drastic measures—the Asylum Cooperative Agreements and the expulsions that it justified on public health grounds—to prevent asylum seekers from entering without even the pretense of an adjudication by U.S. officials. TRAC, https://trac.syr.edu/phptools/immigration/mpp/; Arelis R. Hernandez and Kevin Sieff, *Trump's "Remain in Mexico" Program Dwindles as More Immigrants Are Flown to Guatemala or Are Quickly Deported*," *Washington Post* (Feb. 20, 2020), www.washingtonpost.com/immigration/remain-in-mexico-deportation-asylum-guatemala/2020/02/20/9c29f53e-4eb7-11ea-9b5c-eac5b16dafaa_story.html.

94. Human Rights First, *A Year of Horrors: The Trump Administration's Illegal Returns of Asylum Seekers to Danger in Mexico*, 3 (Jan. 2020).

95. Id.

96. Emily Green, *Trump's Asylum Policies Sent Him Back to Mexico; He Was Kidnapped 5 Hours Later by a Cartel*, Vice News (Sept. 16, 2019), www.vice.com/en_us/article/pa7kkg/trumps-asylum-policies-sent-him-back-to-mexico-he-was-kidnapped-five-hours-later-by-a-cartel.

97. Id.; see also Debbie Nathan, *Trump's "Remain in Mexico" Policy Exposes Migrants to Rape, Kidnapping, and Murder in Dangerous Border Cities*, Intercept (July 14, 2019) (testimonies from a number of immigrants under MPP, including the testimony of an asylum seeker escaping the cartels back home, unable to cross the border to safety because he is stuck in Mexico under MPP, along with a woman and her children who were kidnapped in Juarez); see https://theintercept.com/2019/07/14/trump-remain-in-mexico-policy/.

98. U.S. Department of State, *Mexico Travel Advisory* (June 17, 2020), https://travel.state.gov/content/travel/en/traveladvisories/traveladvisories/mexico-travel-advisory.html; travel advisories for Afghanistan, Syria, and Yemen, https://travel.state.gov/content/travel/en/traveladvisories/traveladvisories.html/.

99. "As of late November 2019, the U.S. Department of Homeland Security sent at least 25,000 individuals to Nuevo Laredo and

Matamoros in the notoriously dangerous state of Tamaulipas, which the U.S. State Department designates as a Level 4 'Do Not Travel,'" the same threat assessment given to Afghanistan, Iran, Libya, and Syria. Since November 2019, the U.S. Consulate in Nuevo Laredo has issued repeated warnings regarding "violence between Mexican authorities and criminal organizations," "multiple gunfights throughout the city of Nuevo Laredo," "blockades on major highways," and "gun battles in various locations" and has reminded U.S. citizens that "organized crime activity (including gun battles, murder, armed robbery, carjacking, kidnapping, forced disappearances, extortion, and sexual assault) is common." Human Rights First, *Year of Horrors*; Human Rights First, *Publicly Reported Cases of Violent Attacks on Individuals Returned to Mexico Under the "Migrant Protection Protocols"* (May 13, 2020), https://perma.cc/72AR-TY2A.

100. Human Rights First, *Year of Horrors*, 3.

101. See Human Rights First, *Delivered to Danger: Illegal Remain in Mexico Policy Imperils Asylum Seekers' Lives and Denies Due Process*, at 17 (Aug. 2019), www.humanrightsfirst.org/sites/default/files/Delivered-to-Danger-August-2019%20.pdf.

102. Debbie Nathan, *U.S. Border Officials Use Fake Addresses, Dangerous Conditions, and Mass Trials to Discourage Asylum-Seekers*, Intercept (Oct. 4, 2019), https://perma.cc/J7QG-4LFK; Adolfo Flores, *Border Patrol Agents Are Writing "Facebook" as a Street Address for Asylum-Seekers Forced to Wait in Mexico* (Sept. 27, 2019), www.buzzfeednews.com/article/adolfoflores/asylum-notice-border-appear-facebook-mexico.

103. At one court session observed by a reporter, only twenty-three of forty-seven migrants appeared. Priscilla Alvarez, *"I Don't Want to Be Deported": Inside the Tent Courts on the U.S.-Mexico Border*, CNN Politics (Jan. 28, 2020), https://perma.cc/4R97-X9JA.

104. TRAC Immigration, *Contrasting Experiences: MPP vs. Non-MPP Immigration Court Cases* (May 28, 2020).

105. The government's official name for its tent courts is "port courts" because they are located near ports of entry. Manny Fernandez, Miriam Jordan, and Caitlin Dickerson, *The Trump*

Administration's Latest Experiment on the Border: Tent Courts,
New York Times (Sept. 12, 2019).

106. Alvarez, *"I Don't Want to Be Deported."*

107. As of November 2019, only 4 percent of migrants in MPP had attorneys, compared with 32 percent of those who remained in the United States for their hearings. TRAC Immigration, Contrasting Experiences, supra.

108. See Alvarez, *"I Don't Want to be Deported,"* reporting on the case of Mikaela Hernandez, who had been to the tent court on four occasions and had been scheduled for a fifth appearance.

109. Michael D. Shear and Ana Swanson, *Trump Says No Deal with Mexico Is Reached as Border Arrests Surge* (June 6, 2019), www.nytimes.com/2019/06/05/us/politics/mexico-tariffs.html.

110. See https://twitter.com/realDonaldTrump/status/11342406 53926232064.

111. U.S. Department of State, *U.S.-Mexico Joint Declaration* (June 7, 2019), https://perma.cc/6X8J-54AC.

112. Maureen Meyer and Adam Isacson, Washington Office on Latin America, *The "Wall" Before the Wall: Mexico's Crackdown on Migration at Its Southern Border,* 4 (Dec. 2019), www.wola.org/wp-content/uploads/2019/12/Mexicos-Southern-Border-2019-FULL-Report.pdf.

113. Id.

114. These figures are drawn from the excellent calculator provided at TRAC Immigration, *Details on MPP (Remain in Mexico) Deportation Proceedings (March 2020),* https://trac.syr.edu/php tools/immigration/mpp/.

115. TRAC, https://trac.syr.edu/phptools/immigration/mpp/; see also Alexandra Kelley, *0.1% of Immigrants Receive Asylum at the Border, The Hill* (Dec. 17, 2019), https://perma.cc/TEQ2 -HHC5.

116. TRAC, https://trac.syr.edu/phptools/immigration/mpp/.

117. Human Rights First, *Year of Horrors,* 5.

118. 8 U.S.C. Sec. 1225(b)(2)(C).

119. For a full explanation of the interaction of these subsections, showing that the provision for requiring certain migrants to have to wait in Mexico does not apply to migrants subject to

expedited removal, see *Innovation Law Lab. v. Wolf,* 951 F. 3rd 1073 (9th Cir., 2020).

120. Order granting preliminary injunction in *Innovation Law Lab, et al., v. Nielsen, Case 3:19-cv-00807* (N.D. Cal.), https://perma .cc/ZK4K-LZ9C.

121. *Innovation Law Lab v. McAleenan*, 924 F. 3rd 503 (9th Cir., 2019).

122. *Innovation Law Lab v. Wolf, et al.* (9th Cir., 2020), 951 F. 3d 1073 (9th Cir. 2020). In addition to construing the words of the statute to bar MPP for asylum seekers who arrived without proper documentation, regardless of whether the Department of Homeland Security decided to put them in regular rather than expedited removal proceedings, the court delved into why Congress adopted the provision requiring some migrants to wait in Mexico and found that it had nothing to do with asylum seekers; section (b)(2)(C) was added to IIRIRA late in the drafting process, in the wake of *Matter of Sanchez-Avila*, 21 I. & N. Dec. 444 (BIA, 1996). Sanchez-Avila was a Mexican national who applied for entry as a "resident alien commuter" but who was charged with being inadmissible due to his "involvement with controlled substances." Id., at 445; see 8 U.S.C. § 1182(a) (2)(A)(i) (§ (b)(2) applicants include aliens who have "violat[ed] . . . any law or regulation . . . relating to a controlled substance"). In order to prevent aliens like Sanchez-Avila from staying in the United States during the pendency of their guaranteed regular removal proceeding under § 1229a, as they would otherwise have a right to do under § (b)(2)(A), Congress added § 1225(b)(2)(C). Congress specifically had in mind undesirable § (b)(2) applicants like Sanchez-Avila. It did not have in mind bona fide asylum seekers under § (b)(1). 951 F. 3rd, at 1087.

123. *Innovation Law Lab et al. v. McAleenan et al.*, Brief of amicus curiae Local 1924 in Support of Plaintiffs-Appellees' Answering Brief and Affirmation of the District Court's Decision, at 3, Case No. 19-15716 (9th Cir., filed June 26, 2019). Ken Cuccinelli, the acting director of USCIS, directly attacked this amicus brief on his Twitter feed. Hamed Aleaziz, *The Top U.S. Asylum*

Official Has Been Pushed Out by the Trump Administration, Buzz-feed News (Sept. 4, 2019), www.buzzfeednews.com/article/hamedaleaziz/uscis-asylum-lafferty-out-reassigned-cuccinelli-trump.

124. *Wolf v. Innovation Law Lab*, U.S. 140 S. Ct. 1564 (2020).

125. *Innovation Law Lab. v. Wolf*, 951 F. 3rd 1073 (9th Cir., 2020), *cert. granted* (U.S. Oct. 29, 2020), No. 19-1212, https://www.supremecourt.gov/orders/courtorders/101920zor_8758.pdf.

126. *Immigrant Defenders Law Center, et al. v. Wolf*, Case No. 2:20-cv-9893 (C.D. Cal., Oct. 28, 2020) https://www.splcenter.org/sites/default/files/complaint_dkt_1-_immigrant_defenders_law_center_et_al_v._wolf_et_al.pdf.

127. U.S. Department of Justice, *Interim Final Rule: Asylum Eligibility and Procedural Modifications*, 84 *Fed. Reg.* 33,829 (July 16, 2019). It exempts Mexican nationals and victims of a severe form of human trafficking. Id.; Human Rights First, *Trump Administration's Third-Country Transit Bar Is an Asylum Ban That Will Return Refugees to Danger*, 1 (Sept. 2019), www.humanrightsfirst.org/sites/default/files/Third-Country-Transit-Ban.pdf.

128. The Trump administration issued guidance to asylum officers interpreting the "significant possibility" test to require the applicant to "demonstrate a substantial and realistic possibility of succeeding." USCIS, *Lesson Plan Overview, Credible Fear of Persecution and Torture Determinations*, at 12 (Apr. 19, 2019), linked from www.aila.org/infonet/uscis-updates-officer-training-credible-fear.

129. Human Rights First, *Asylum Denied Families Divided: Trump Administration's Illegal Third-Country Transit Ban*, 2, 4 (July 2020), www.humanrightsfirst.org/resource/asylum-denied-families-divided-trump-administration-s-illegal-third-country-transit-ban.

130. Id.

131. Id.

132. 8 U.S.C. § 1158(b)(2)(A)(vi).

133. 8 U.S.C. § 1158(a)(2)(A).

134. 8 C.F.R. § 208.15.

135. U.S.-Canada Safe Third Country Agreement (2002) (navigate to "View the live page"). As discussed further below, in July 2020, a Canadian federal court held that the United States–Canada agreement violated Section 7 of the Canadian Charter (Constitution), the right to life, liberty, and security of the person. *The Canadian Council for Refugees, et. al v. The Minister of Immigration, et. al*, 2020 FC 77 (July 22, 2020). The court suspended the effect of its decision for six months to allow time for the Parliament to respond.

136. 8 U.S.C. Sec. 1158(b)(2)(C).

137. *East Bay Sanctuary Covenant v. Barr*, 385 F. Supp. 3rd 922, 938–57 (N.D. Cal., 2019).

138. *Barr v. East Bay Sanctuary Covenant*, 588 U.S. 140 S. Ct. 3 (2019).

139. *Barr v. East Bay Sanctuary Covenant*, 588 U.S. 140 S. Ct. 3 (2019) (Sotomayor, J, dissenting). In a separate lawsuit challenging the Third Country Transit Bar, another federal district court blocked the Trump administration from applying that bar to those who first sought entry before its effective date. *Al Otro Lado v. McAleenan*, 423 F. Supp. 3rd 848 (S.D. Calif., 2019).

140. *East Bay Sanctuary Covenant v. Barr*, 964 F. 3rd 832 (9th Cir., 2020). The government moved for rehearing en banc (by all of the judges on the Ninth Circuit) on October 5, 2020.

141. *Capital Area Immigrant Rights Coalition v. Trump*, 2020 U.S. Dist. Lexis 114421 (D.D.C. 2020), https://ecf.dcd.uscourts.gov /cgi-bin/show_public_doc?2019cv2117-72.

142. The final TCTB rule, published on December 17, 2020, and effective January 19, 2021, can be found at DOJ and DHS, *Asylum Eligibility and Procedural Modifications*, 85 Fed. Reg. 82260 (Dec. 17, 2020).

143. 8 U.S.C. § 1158(a)(2)(A).

144. See the U.S-Canada Safe Third Country Agreement; Democratic Staff Report Prepared for the use of the Committee on Foreign Relations, United States Senate, *Cruelty, Coercion, and Legal Contortion: The Trump Administration's Unsafe Asylum Cooperative Agreements with Guatemala, Honduras, and El Salvador* 5-6 (Jan. 18, 2021), https://www.foreign.senate.gov/imo/me dia/doc/Cruelty,%20Coercion,%20and%20Legal%20Contor tions%20--%20SFRC%20Democratic%20Staff%20Report.pdf

145. Adam Isacson, Washington Office on Latin America, Commentary, *"I Can't Believe What's Happening—What We're Becoming": A Memo from El Paso and Ciudad Juarez* (Dec. 29, 2019), https://perma.cc/F9Q3-F5E3.

146. John Wagner, Mary Beth Sheridan, David J. Lynch, and Maria Sacchetti, *Trump Threatens Guatemala After It Backs Away from "Safe Third Country" Asylum Deal*, Washington Post (July 23, 2019), www.washingtonpost.com/politics/trump-threatens -guatemala-over-delay-in-safe-third-country-asylum-deal /2019/07/23/cc22417e-ad45-11e9-bc5c-e73b603e7f38_ story.html.

147. U.S. Department of Homeland Security, *Fact Sheet: DHS Agreements with Guatemala, Honduras, and El Salvador*, www .dhs.gov/sites/default/files/publications/19_1028_opa_fact sheet-northern-central-america-agreements_v2.pdf.

148. The three have ranked toward the top of the global lists of countries with respect to homicides and femicides per capita. See the text in chapter 2 at pages 26 and 29 and the corresponding notes 35 and 51–53, Democratic Staff Report Prepared for the use of the Committee on Foreign Relations, United States Senate, *Cruelty, Coercion, and Legal Contortion: The Trump Administration's Unsafe Asylum Cooperative Agreements with Guatemala, Honduras, and El Salvador* 6-7 (Jan. 18, 2021), https:// www.foreign.senate.gov/imo/media/doc/Cruelty,%20Coer cion,%20and%20Legal%20Contortions%20--%20SFRC%20 Democratic%20Staff%20Report.pdf .

149. U.S. Citizenship and Immigration Services, *Implementing Bilateral and Multilateral Asylum Cooperative Agreements Under the Immigration and Nationality Act*, 84 Fed. Reg. 63994 (Nov. 19, 2019).

150. The Guatemalan Constitutional Court first issued an injunction against the president of Guatemala proceeding with the ACA. Two months later, that court rescinded the injunction but raised questions about legal compliance issues that could arise under the Constitution depending on how the president proceeded with the ACA. Refugees International and Human Rights Watch, *Deportation with a Layover: Failure of Protection under the U.S.-Guatemala Asylum Cooperative Agreement*, 11

(May 2020), https://perma.cc/FF67-XBEF. On December 15, 2020, DHS announced that the United States and El Salvador had completed the implementation accords for the ACA. This step now allows the U.S. to remove asylum seekers to El Salvador. DHS, *El Salvador Begins Implementation of Asylum Cooperative Agreement,* (Dec. 15, 2020), https://perma.cc /G4RB-3454.

151. *Agreement Between the Government of the United States of America and the Government of the Republic of Guatemala on Cooperation Regarding the Examination of Protection Claims,* U.S. Department of Homeland Security, 84 *Fed. Reg.* 64095 (Nov. 20, 2019). Nothing in the agreement or the interim final rule implementing it limits the application of the agreement to citizens of the Northern Triangle. Indeed, it appears that the Trump administration planned to phase in the transfer of Mexican nationals to Guatemala. Mica Rosenberg, *U.S. Implements Plan to Send Mexican Asylum Seekers to Guatemala,* Reuters (Jan. 6, 2020), www.reuters.com/article/us-usa-immigration /u-s-implements-plan-to-send-mexican-asylum seekers-to-gua temala-idUSKBN1Z51S4. The Honduras and El Salvador agreements, if implemented, could apply to Nicaraguans, Cubans, and possibly other groups, either instead of or in addition to individuals from the Northern Triangle. See David C. Adams and Jorge Cancino, *Honduras Agrees to Be "Safe Third Country" for Cubans and Nicaraguans,* Univision (Sept. 9, 2019), 84 *Fed. Reg.* 63994, www.univision.com/univision-news/immigration /honduras-agrees-to-be-safe-third-country-for-cubans-and-ni caraguans.

152. After the Trump administration ordered asylum and other protection officers to carry out policies that forced asylum seekers to wait in Mexico or deported them to Guatemala, one such officer refused to do that and left the Department of Homeland Security: "I joined the government to be a protection officer," she said. But with her new assignments, "there was a high chance we would place someone in danger, and I was not comfortable being a part of that." Zolan Kanno-Youngs and Emily Cochrane, *Immigration Officers Face Furloughs as Visa Ap-*

plications Plunge, New York Times (July 3, 2020), www.nytimes
.com/2020/07/03/us/politics/immigration-furloughs-coro
navirus.html?searchResultPosition=1.

153. *Letter to Secretary of State Michael Pompeo et al. from Sen. Eliz-abeth Warren and 20 Other Senators* (Feb. 5, 2020), https://
perma.cc/SEZ9-MMJM.

154. Refugees International, *Deportation with a Layover*.

155. Kevin Sieff, "The U.S. Is Putting Asylum Seekers on Planes to
Guatemala—Often Without Telling Them Where They're Go-ing," *Washington Post* (Jan. 14, 2020).

156. Refugees International, *Deportation with a Layover*.

157. Id.; Georgetown Law Human Rights Institute, *Dead End: No
Path To Protection for Asylum Seekers Under the Guatemala Asy-lum Cooperative Agreement*, 50 (June 2020), https://perma.cc
/73BY-4Z4K.

158. Human Rights First, *Is Guatemala Safe for Refugees and Asylum
Seekers?* (July 1, 2019), https://perma.cc/7HAR-KKDZ.

159. Georgetown Law Human Rights Institute, *Dead End*.

160. See Georgetown Law Human Rights Institute, press release
for *Dead End: No Path To Protection for Asylum Seekers Under
the Guatemala Asylum Cooperative Agreement* (June 10, 2020),
https://perma.cc/4LBP-ZBW8.

161. Id.

162. Id.

163. Complaint, *U.T. v. Barr (Case 1:20-cv-00116, D.D.C. 2020)*,
https://perma.cc/5E8C-GZLE, Democratic Staff Report Pre-pared for the use of the Committee on Foreign Relations, United
States Senate, *Cruelty, Coercion, and Legal Contortion: The
Trump Administration's Unsafe Asylum Cooperative Agreements
with Guatemala, Honduras, and El Salvador* (Jan. 18, 2021),
https://www.foreign.senate.gov/imo/media/doc/Cruelty,
%20Coercion,%20and%20Legal%20Contortions%20--%20
SFRC%20Democratic%20Staff%20Report.pdf.

164. Id. On March 16, 2020, deportations to Guatemala under the
ACA were temporarily suspended in response to the COVID-19
pandemic. By that point, the United States had removed 939
people to Guatemala. The deportations resumed but were sus-

pended again in April after seventy returnees tested positive for the coronavirus. NPR, *Guatemala Suspends Deportations from U.S. After 70 Test Positive for Coronavirus* (Apr. 17, 2020). They resumed again in June 2020. Associated Press, U.S. *Resumes Deportation Flights to Guatemala After Month-Long Suspension*, *Time* (June 10, 2020), https://time.com/5851118/guatemala-deportations-u-s-immigration/.

165. 8 U.S.C. Sec. 1158(a)(2)(A).

166. *Memorandum from Attorney General William Barr, Nov. 7, 2019*, in *Defendants' Appendix Under Local Civil Rule 7(n)(1)*, at 633 (Mar. 27, 2020), in *U.T. v. Barr*, https://perma.cc/BDK9-SK4K.

167. The Guatemalan "representations" assert, e.g., that "Guatemala's protection application capacity information improved after the rules for the determination and granting of refugee status, adopted in March, 2019, took effect." Untitled representations from the Government of Guatemala, attached to *Memorandum from Attorney General William Barr*, id., at 636. The representations do not say what the "application capacity" is or that the *adjudication* capacity is adequate to serve the expected or potential number of people removed to Guatemala under the ACA.

168. Twenty-one U.S. senators complained to Secretary of State Michael Pompeo and other senior Trump administration officials that "the notion that Guatemala or the other two Northern Triangle countries offers such a procedure strains credulity—their systems for determining asylum claims are, at best, deeply flawed and under-resourced, and at worst, practically non-existent. . . . Guatemala does not have a dedicated office for resolving asylum cases; instead, a commission of four officials from several ministries and the immigration department meet a few times a year to decide cases. Reportedly, these officials did not resolve a single case in the first seven months of 2019." *Letter to Secretary Michael Pompeo*, supra n. 153, at 3.

169. Complaint, *U.T. v. Barr*, supra n. 166.

170. Attorney General Sessions, *Remarks to the Executive Office for Immigration Review* (Oct. 12, 2017), https://perma.cc/KZU4-8AQM.

171. See *First Amended Complaint for Declaratory and Injunctive Relief, Las Americas v. Wolf*, at ¶ 70, (Dec. 5, 2019), (hereafter *PACR Complaint*), https://perma.cc/QU52-4F3Q.

172. Tanvi Misra and Camila DeChalus, *DHS Expands Programs That Fast-Track Asylum Process*, Roll Call (Feb. 26, 2020), https://perma.cc/T489-CQST. Unaccompanied children and persons with serious or imminent health concerns are exempt from this program. *Attachment D: Streamlined Processing Procedures and Third Country Pilot Guidelines, Administrative Record, Las Americas v. Wolf*, at AR 640–41 (Jan. 27, 2020), (hereafter *PACR Pilot Guidelines*).

173. *PACR Pilot Guidelines*, at AR 641.

174. *PACR Complaint*, at ¶ 172–80, https://perma.cc/QU52 -4F3Q; *Plaintiff's Statement of Undisputed Material Facts, Las Americas v. Wolf*, at ¶ 90; (Jan. 27, 2020), Robert Moore, *Trump Administration Testing Rapid Asylum Review Deportation Process in Texas, Washington Post* (Oct. 24, 2019).

175. *Plaintiff's Statement of Undisputed Material Facts*, at ¶ 1.

176. Human Rights First, *Grant Rates Plummet as Trump Administration Dismantles U.S. Asylum System, Blocks and Deports Refugees*, 7 (June 2020), www.humanrightsfirst.org/sites/default/files /AdministrationDismantlingUSAsylumSystem.pdf.

177. Internal guidance implementing PACR/HARP initially indicated that individuals would receive only "one calendar day" to consult before having their CFI, consistent with a July 2019 memorandum written by acting USCIS Director Cuccinelli changing the long-standing 48-hour minimum policy to a 24-hour minimum. *PACR Pilot Guidelines*, at AR 641. However, as of March 2020, the Department of Homeland Security has restored the initial 48-hour policy pursuant to *L.M.-M. v. Cuccinelli*, which struck down the Cuccinelli memorandum because his appointment as USCIS director was defective. *Declaration of Ashley B. Caudill-Mirillo, Las Americas v. Wolf*, May 4, 2020, at ¶ 6–10.

178. *PACR Pilot Guidelines*, at AR 641. Although the guidelines do not specify how much time an individual is given to contact family members, plaintiffs report a short time frame of 30

minutes to an hour in which they were given access to a phone. *PACR Complaint*, at ¶ 8, 177.

179. *Statement of Undisputed Material Facts*, at ¶ 17–27, 42, 111.

180. *PACR Complaint*, at ¶ 9.

181. *PACR Pilot Guidelines*, at AR 642. At least one individual had their CFI through a cell phone while in the hielera. *PACR Complaint*, at ¶ 178. It is implied that these CFIs are conducted by Asylum Officers, not CBP officers, but it is not entirely clear.

182. *PACR Pilot Guidelines*, at AR 642.

183. Id.

184. *Statement of Undisputed Material Facts*, at ¶112–21.

185. *PACR Pilot Guidelines*, at AR 642–643; Moore, *Trump Administration Testing*.

186. *PACR Complaint*, at ¶ 10.

187. Misra and DeChalus, *DHS Expands Programs*; *PACR Pilot Guidelines*, at AR 641.

188. Misra and DeChalus, *DHS Expands Programs*, at ¶ 15–16. Early on in the program, a Mexican man was held at a CBP facility for three weeks, seemingly in connection with a HARP procedure. Max Rivlin-Nadler, *Asylum Seeker Held Incommunicado for Three Weeks by Border Patrol*, KPBS (Nov. 26, 2019), www.kpbs.org/news/2019/nov/26/asylum-seeker-held-incommunicado-three-weeks-border/.

189. *PACR Pilot Guidelines*, at AR 643; Moore, *Trump Administration Testing*.

190. Misra and DeChalus, *DHS Expands Programs*.

191. In June 2019, 98 percent of the families detained at the so-called Family Residential Centers met the credible fear standard; by February 2020, that had fallen to 30 percent. The vast majority of the detained families are nationals of El Salvador, Guatemala, and Honduras. USCIS, *Semi-Monthly Credible Fear and Reasonable Fear Receipts and Decisions*, www.uscis.gov/tools/reports-studies/immigration-forms-data/semi-monthly-credible-fear-and-reasonable-fear-receipts-and-decisions; Human Rights First, *Grant Rates Plummet*.

192. Hernandez and Sieff, *Trump's "Remain in Mexico" Program Dwindles*.

193. See, generally, *PACR Complaint* and *Plaintiffs' Memorandum of Law in Support of Motion for Summary Judgment, Las Americas v. Wolf*, No. 19-cv-3640 (Jan. 27, 2020).

194. 8 U.S.C. § 1225(b)(1)(B)(iv): "An alien who is eligible for such interview may consult with a person or persons of the alien's choosing prior to the interview or any review thereof, according to regulations prescribed by the Attorney General. Such consultation shall be at no expense to the Government and shall not unreasonably delay the process."

195. 8 C.F.R. § 208.30(d)(4): "The alien may consult with a person or persons of the alien's choosing prior to the interview or any review thereof, and may present other evidence, if available. Such consultation shall be at no expense to the Government and shall not unreasonably delay the process. Any person or persons with whom the alien chooses to consult may be present at the interview and may be permitted, in the discretion of the asylum officer, to present a statement at the end of the interview."

196. "In any removal proceedings before an immigration judge and in any appeal proceedings before the Attorney General from any such removal proceedings, the person concerned shall have the privilege of being represented (at no expense to the Government) by such counsel, authorized to practice in such proceedings, as he shall choose." 8 U.S.C. § 1362. "A person compelled to appear in person before an agency or representative thereof" has the right "to be accompanied, represented, and advised by counsel." 5 U.S.C. § 555(b). Federal courts have held that the right to counsel in the INA does not apply to CFI/RFI interviews not before an immigration judge. See, e.g., *U.S. v. Barajas-Alvarado*, 655 F. 3rd 1077, 1088 (9th Cir., 2011): "The cases cited by Barajas–Alvarado involve aliens in the more formal removal proceedings, where the regulations provide a right of counsel, as compared to expedited removal proceedings, where they do not." However, other courts have held that the APA provides a right to counsel in some contexts where the INA does not. *Doe v. Wolf*, 19-cv-2119-DMS, 2020 WL 209100, at *5 (S.D. Cal., Jan. 14, 2020) (finding a right to counsel for MPP nonrefoulement interviews).

197. *PACR Complaint*, at ¶ 191–206. The question of whether the governing statutes and regulations guarantee in-person attorney access was recently addressed in another case. *Doe v. Wolf*, 2020 WL 209100, at *5 (holding that the use of the word "accompanied" in the APA right to counsel provision connotes in-person presence).

198. *Plaintiffs' Memorandum of Law in Support of Motion for Summary Judgment*, at 16–32, 39–40. Cf. *Dept. of Homeland Security v. Regents of the Univ. of Calif.*, U. S. 140 S. Ct. 1891 (2020) invalidating the rescission of the Obama-created program of Deferred Action for Childhood Arrivals (DACA) because the Department of Homeland Security did not provide a sufficiently well-reasoned explanation for the rescission, as required by the Administrative Procedures Act.

199. Memorandum Opinion, *Las Americas v. Wolf*, No. 19-cv-3640 (D. D.C., Nov. 30, 2020); *Las Americas v. Wolf*, Case 20-5386 (D.C. Cir.) (appeal).

200. Caitlin Dickerson and Michael D. Shear, *Before Covid-19, Trump Aide Sought to Use Disease to Close Border*, New York Times (May 3, 2020), https://www.nytimes.com/2020/05/03/us/corona virus-immigration-stephen-miller-public-health.html?action= click&module=RelatedLinks&pgtype=Article.

201. Centers for Disease Control and Prevention, *Order Suspending Introduction of Certain Persons from Countries Where a Communicable Disease Exists*, at 1 (Mar. 20, 2020), https://perma .cc/2ZAT-T85N; Quinn Owen, *Trump Administration to Impose New Restrictions at Border, Leaving Asylum Seekers in Limbo*, ABC News (Mar. 20, 2020), https://perma.cc/3VHF-4PR9.

202. Pence's senior aide, Olivia Troye, resigned in protest, "saying the administration had placed politics above public health." Jason Dearen and Garance Burke, *VP Pence Ordered Borders Closed After CDC Experts Refused*, Minnesota Star Tribune (Oct. 3, 2020), www.startribune.com/vp-pence-ordered-borders-closed-after -cdc-experts-refused/572622611/; Union of Concerned Scientists, *CDC Scientists Sidelined in Decision to Seal U.S. Border* (Oct. 19, 2020), https://www.ucsusa.org/resources/attacks-on-sci ence/cdc-scientists-sidelined-decision-seal-us-border.

203. *Order Suspending Introduction of Certain Persons*, at 1–2.

204. Id., at 2.

205. Id., at 6–10.

206. Id., at 10.

207. Id., at 11–12.

208. Id., at 12.

209. Id., at 16.

210. Id., at 17.

211. Department of Health and Human Services, *Amendment and Extension of Order Suspending Introduction of Certain Persons from Countries Where a Communicable Disease Exists* (May 19, 2020), https://perma.cc/4RKS-HVTP.

212. *Control of Communicable Diseases; Foreign Quarantine: Suspension of Introduction of Persons into United States from Designated Foreign Countries or Places for Public Health Purposes*, 85 *Fed. Reg.* 16559 (Mar. 24, 2020), www.govinfo.gov/content/pkg /FR-2020-03-24/pdf/2020-06238.pdf.

213. 42 U.S.C. § 265; Id., at 16560.

214. 42 U.S.C. § 264.

215. 85 *Fed. Reg.* 16560.

216. Id., at 16563.

217. Id., at 16564.

218. Dara Lind, *Leaked Border Patrol Memo Tells Agents to Send Migrants Back Immediately—Ignoring Asylum Law* (Apr. 2, 2020) (includes link to CBP guidance).

219. Id.

220. 8 U.S.C. Sec. 1231(b)(3). The exception for humanitarian and public safety considerations requires approval by the chief agent in a given sector and seems to be applied mostly to people who CBP determines should be detained because they are dangerous rather than for people who are ill or at risk. Lind, *Leaked Border Patrol Memo*.

221. *Letter to Alex Azar, HHS Secretary, and Robert Redfield, from Leaders of Public Health Schools, Medical Schools, Hospitals, and Other U.S. Institutions* (May 18, 2020), www.publichealth .columbia.edu/public-health-now/news/public-health-ex perts-urge-us-officials-withdraw-order-enabling-mass-expu lsion-asylum-seekers.

222. Migration Policy Institute, *Crisis Within a Crisis: Immigration*

in the United States in a Time of COVID-19 (Mar. 26, 2020), www.migrationpolicy.org/article/crisis-within-crisis-immigra tion-time-covid-19.

223. U.S. Department of Homeland Security, press release, *Department of Homeland Security and Department of Justice Announce Plan to Restart MPP Hearings* (July 17, 2020), www.dhs.gov /news/2020/07/17/department-homeland-security-and-de partment-justice-announce-plan-restart-mpp.

224. Jonathan O'Connell, Erica Werner, and Aaron Gregg, *First Coronavirus Case Identified at Largest Migrant Camp on U.S.-Mexico Border, Washington Post* (June 30, 2020), www.washing tonpost.com/nation/2020/06/30/coronavirus-live-updates -us/#link-XC5HJOUOGFC7LPDGAI72WHGPE4.

225. U.S. Customs and Border Protection, *Nationwide Enforcement Encounters: Title 8 Enforcement Actions and Title 42 Expulsions*, www.cbp.gov/newsroom/stats/cbp-enforcement-statistics /title-8-and-title-42-statistics. The data in this paragraph are all found on this CBP website. "Expulsion" is the term used by CBP to refer to COVID-19 removals. The term does not appear in either Title 42, Section 265, or the HHS rule, which authorizes the CDC director to "suspend the introduction of persons" into the United States. See www.govinfo.gov/content /pkg/FR-2020-03-24/pdf/2020-06238.pdf.

226. Camilo Montoya-Galvez, *Texas detention facility becomes staging ground for expulsions of migrant families with children*, CBS News, (October 29, 2020), https://www.cbsnews.com/news/ice-mi grant-families-expulsion-karnes-city-texas-detention-center/.

227. Id.; Caitlin Dickerson, *10 Years Old, Tearful and Confused After a Sudden Deportation, New York Times* (May 21, 2020); Felipe De La Hoz, *Citing the Pandemic, CBP Has Expelled Newborn U.S. Citizens With Their Migrant Mothers, The Intercep* (Jan. 2, 2021); Human Rights First, *Pandemic as Pretext: Trump Administration Exploits COVID-19, Expels Asylum Seekers and Children to Escalating Danger* (2020), https://perma.cc/CE3G-5NLT.; Memorandum Opinion, *P.J.E.S. v Wolf*, Civ. Action No. 20-2245 (D. D.C. 2020).

228. Michael R. Pompeo, secretary of state, "The United States Con-

demns the Ortega Regime's Attack on the Free Press" (Sept. 15, 2020), www.state.gov/the-united-states-condemns-the-ortega -regimes-attack-on-the-free-press/.

229. Kevin Sieff, *She Fled Detention and Torture in Nicaragua for Asylum in the United States; The Government Put Her on a Plane Back Home, Washington Post* (Aug. 28, 2020), www.washingtonpost.com/world /the_americas/nicaragua-asylum-us-border/2020/08/27/9aa ba414-e561-11ea-970a-64c73a1c2392_story.html.

230. Id.

231. Caitlin Dickerson, *U.S. Expels Migrant Children from Other Countries to Mexico, New York Times* (Oct. 30, 2020).

232. Nick Miroff, *Under Coronavirus Immigration Measures, U.S. Is Expelling Border-Crossers to Mexico in an Average of 96 Minutes, Washington Post* (Mar. 30, 2020).

233. Customs and Border Protection, *Southwest Border Migration 2020,* https://perma.cc/FN64-3BXC; Customs and Border Protection, *Southwest Border Migration 2019,* https://perma .cc/L4N6-46B9.

234. Customs and Border Protection, *Southwest Border Migration FY 2020,* https://perma.cc/V35H-42ST; see Elliot Spagat, *Border Authorities Use Pandemic Powers to Expel Immigrants,* ABC News (July 10, 2020), https://perma.cc/G5LF-ZJW7: "Most of the people crossing the border illegally are now Mexican adults—a change from the recent past, when they were predominantly Central American families and children."

235. Lucas Guttentag, *Coronavirus Border Expulsions: CDC's Assault on Asylum Seekers and Unaccompanied Minors, Just Security* (Apr. 13, 2020), https://perma.cc/VTT8-7PJL.

236. Id.

237. Id.

238. Department of Health and Human Services, *Control of Communicable Diseases; Foreign Quarantine: Suspension of the Right to Introduce and Prohibition of Introduction of Persons into United States from Designated Foreign Countries or Places for Public Health Purposes,* 85 Fed. Reg. 56424 (Sept. 11, 2020), https:// www.govinfo.gov/content/pkg/FR-2020-09-11/pdf/2020 -20036.pdf. The rule became effective on Oct. 13, 2020.

239. Id., at 56425.
240. Department of Homeland Security and Department of Justice, "Security Bars and Processing," 85 *Fed. Reg.* 41201 (July 9, 2020), www.govinfo.gov/content/pkg/FR-2020-07-09/pdf/2020-14758.pdf; 85 Fed. Reg. 84160 (Dec. 23, 2020), https://www.govinfo.gov/content/pkg/FR-2020-12-23/pdf/2020-28436.pdf..
241. Scott Roehm, *Trump's Latest Assault on Asylum Has Nothing to Do with National Security or Public Health* (July 15, 2020), www.justsecurity.org/71422/trumps-latest-assault-on-asylum-has-nothing-to-do-with-national-security-or-public-health/.
242. *Letter to Department of Homeland Security Secretary Chad Wolf and Attorney General William Barr from Leaders of Public Health Schools, Medical Schools, Hospitals, and Other U.S. Institutions* (Aug. 6, 2020), https://perma.cc/A742-C5CW.
243. Id.

Chapter 5

1. The proposed rule appears as Depts. of Homeland Security and Justice, *Procedures for Asylum and Withholding of Removal*, 85 *Fed. Reg.* 36264 (June 15, 2020). The final rule appears as Dept's of Homeland Security and Justice, *Procedures for Asylum and Withholding of Removal*, 85 Fed. Reg. 80274 (Dec, 11, 2020). The preliminary injunction that stopped the rule from going into effect as scheduled on January 11, 2021, is reported as *Pangea Legal Services v. Dept. of Homeland Security*, 2021 U.S. Dist. LEXIS 5093 (N.D. Ca. 2021).
2. Refugee, Asylum, and International Operations Directorate Training, Asylum Division Officer Training Course, *Credible Fear of Persecution and Torture Determinations*, 31 (Apr. 30, 2019), https://perma.cc/6AVZ-ZM53.
3. 8 *C.F.R.* Sec. 208.30(e)(1)(iii), as amended by the new regulation. If the preliminary injunction in *Pangea Legal Services*, discussed in the text, ripens into a permanent injunction or in vacation of the regulation, or if the Biden administration negotiates a settlement of that case or amends the regulation, the sections

of the Code of Federal Regulations that are cited in this and the following endnotes may be withdrawn or modified.

4. This also applies to other bars, such as the firm resettlement bar, and to any bars that an overreaching executive branch might impose in the future.

5. *Matter of E-F-H-L-*, 27 I. & N. Dec. 226 (A.G., 2018).

6. 8 C. F. R. Sec. 1208.13(e)(1), (2), as amended by the new regulation. The regulation requires the judge to give the respondent ten days notice of an intention to deny asylum without a hearing. Id.

7. See, e.g., Jeffrey S. Chase, *The AG's Strange Decision in Matter of E-F-H-L* (blog, Mar. 10, 2018).

8. *Hernandez-Chacon v. Barr*, 948 F. 3rd 94 (2d Cir., 2020). See also *Matter of R. G. Immig. Ct. Hartford, Ct.* (Nov. 14, 2017), https://drive.google.com/file/d/1Q2Xpf9ASsZ88mTBbOiVFm1RcYS0N3UPD/edit; and the unpublished immigration court decisions from El Paso, San Antonio, and Los Angeles reported by Capital Area Immigrants' Rights Coalition, *Seeking Asylum from Gang-Based Violence in Central America: A Resource Manual*, at 18–19 (2007), https://perma.cc/3J9M-CMMZ. Immigration court opinions are rarely published or even transcribed, so the rate of success on such claims is impossible to determine.

9. 8 *C.F.R.* Sec. 208.1(d), 1201.8 (d), as amended by the new regulation.

10. See chapter 3.

11. 8 *C.F.R.* Sec. 208.1(f)(1)(ii), 1208.1(f)(1)(ii), as amended by the new regulation.

12. 8 *C.F.R.* Sec. 208.13(b)(3), 1208.13(b)(3), as amended by the new regulation.

13. *De Pena-Paniagua v. Barr*, 957 F. 3rd 88 (1st Cir., 2020). The court remanded the case to the Board of Immigration Appeals, however, because the formulation of women as a social group had been raised by amicus Center for Gender and Refugee Studies on appeal to the court, and the board had therefore not fully considered it.

14. 8 *C.F.R.* 208.1(f)(1)(viii), 1208.1(f)(viii), as amended by the new regulation. For extra measure, the rule adds that judges

should deny a claim based on "interpersonal disputes of which governmental authorities were unaware or uninvolved," so that women who do not report domestic or gang violence to the police, when the police never act on such complaints because they are in the pay of or afraid of the persecutor, are rendered ineligible for asylum by this provision as well as others. 8 *C.F.R.* Sec. 208.1 (c), 1208.1(c), as amended by the new regulation.

15. See, e.g., Karen Musalo, *El Salvador: A Peace Worse Than War*, 30 *Yale J. L. and Feminism* 3, 25–45 (2018).

16. 8 *C.F.R.* Sec. 208.1(g), 1208.1(g), as amended by the new regulation.

17. *Matter of Toboso-Alfonso*, 20 I. & N. 819 (1990), designated as constituting a precedent by the attorney general in 1994. See David Johnston, *Ruling Backs Homosexuals on Asylum*, *New York Times* (June 17, 1994).

18. *Bostock v. Clayton County*, 590 U.S. 140 S. Ct. 1731 (2020).

19. U.S. Citizenship and Immigration Services, RAIO Directorate, Definition of Persecution and Eligibility Based on Past Conduct (training manual) (Dec. 20, 2019), https://perma.cc/TR5Z -4PT8.

20. See *Crespin-Valladares v. Holder*, 632 F. 3rd 117, 126 (4th Cir., 2011).

21. 8 *C.F.R.* Sec. 208.1(e), 1208.1(e), as amended by the new regulation.

22. See chapter 4.

23. 8 *C.F.R.* Sec. 208.18(a)(1), 1208.18(a)(1) by the new regulation.

24. Between the issuance of the proposed rule and the promulgation of the final rule, the attorney general decided, in a case he had certified to himself, that torture by police officials qualifies as torture under color of law, rendering the victim eligible for relief under the Convention Against Torture, even if the police officials had not been authorized to engage in torture.. *Matter of O-F-A-S-* , 28 I. & N. Dec. 35 (A.G., July 14, 2020).

25. *Matter of Pula*, 19 I. & N. Dec. 467 (BIA, 1987).

26. Id., 474.

27. 8 *C.F.R.* Sec. 208.13(d)(1), 1208.13(d)(1), as amended by the new regulation.

28. 8 *C.F.R.* Sec. 208.13(d)(1)(i), 1208.13(d)(1)(i), as amended by the new regulation.

29. 8 *C.F.R.* Sec. 208.13(d)(1)(ii), 1208.13(d)(1)(ii), as amended by the new regulation.

30. 8 *C.F.R.* Sec. 208.1(d)(2)(i)(A) and (B); 8 *C.F.R.* Sec. 1208.1(d)(2)(i)(A) and (B), as amended by the new regulation.

31. 8 *C.F.R.* Sec 208.1(d)(2)(ii), 1208.1(d)(2)(ii), as amended by the new regulation.

32. *Matter of A-G-G-*, 25 I. & N. Dec. 486, 492–93 (BIA, 2011).

33. 8 *C.F.R.* Sec. 208.15 prior to the 2020 amendment. See also *Matter of A-G-G-*, 25 I. & N. Dec. 486 (BIA, 2011).

34. 8 *C.F.R.* Sec. 208.15(a)(1) and (2), as amended by the new regulation.

35. "Information contained in or pertaining to any asylum application . . . shall not be disclosed without the written consent of the applicant except as permitted by this section or at the discretion of the Attorney General." The exceptions in the section allowed disclosure to a U.S. government official with a need to examine the application. 8 *C.F.R.* Sec. 1208.6(a) prior to amendment.

36. 8 *C.F.R.* Sec. 1208.6(d)(1)(i), as amended by the new regulation.

37. Dept's of Homeland Security and Justice, *Procedures for Asylum and Withholding of Removal*, 85 Fed. Reg., 80274, 80284 (Dec. 11, 2020)

38. Zolan Kanno-Youngs, *Asylum Officers Condemn What They Call "Draconian" Plans by Trump*, New York Times (July 15, 2020).

39. Natalie Nanasi, *New Trump Immigration Regulations Would Devastate Refugee* Pathways, The Hill (June 16, 2020). Two of the authors are directors of Georgetown Law School's asylum law clinic and collectively have forty-five years of experience representing asylum seekers. Nanasi's observation applies to their representation as well.

40. *Pangea Legal Services v. Dept. of Homeland Security,* Case 20-9253 (N.D. Ca. 2021).

41. *Batalla Vidal v. Wolf,* 2020 WL 6695076 (E.D.N.Y. 2020); *North-*

west Immigrant Rights Coalition v. USCIS, 2020 WL 5995206 (D. D.C. 2020); *Immigrant Legal Res. Ctr. v. Wolf,* 2020 WL 5798269 (N.D. Cal. 2020); *Casa de Maryland v. Wolf,* 2020 WL.

42. Nick Miroff and Carol D. Leonnig, *Chad Wolf Resigns as Homeland Security Secretary, Washingoton Post* (Jan. 11, 2021).

43. Order Designating the Order of Succession for the Secretary of Homeland Security, signed by Chad Wolf as Acting Secretary, January 11, 2021; DHS Delegation No. 23028, Jan. 14, 2021; Michael D. Shear, *Trump and Aides Drove Family Separation at the Border, Documents Say, New York Times* (Jan. 14, 2021).

44. *Dept. of Homeland Security Ratification of Actions Taken by the Acting Secretary of Homeland Security,* signed by Chad Wolf on Jan. 16, 2021; *Motion for Reconsideration in Pangea Legal Services v. Dept. of Homeland Security* (Jan. 19, 2021).

45. As John Oliver put it, "The Trump administration's attack on this system has just been relentless, and there are lives at stake here." *Asylum: Last Week Tonight with John Oliver* (Oct. 25, 2020), https://www.youtube.com/watch?v=xtdU5RPDZqI.

46. The form is known as DHS Form I-589.

47. See proposed Form I-589, OMB 1615-0067 (Sept. 30, 2012).

48. An affirmative answer, which would likely be required of anyone from El Salvador or Honduras who passed through Guatemala and Mexico, would trigger the omnibus regulation's provision that the government would not look with favor on applicants who had passed through two or more countries.

49. E.g., this ninety-four-word sentence: "If the entity or person(s) who cause the harm was not the government or a government actor, explain whether the government or a public official acting in an official capacity or other person acting in an official capacity had awareness of the harm, how the government or a public official acting in an official capacity or other person acting in an official capacity became aware of the harm, and whether the government or a public official acting in an official capacity or other person acting in an official capacity acted to prevent such harm."

50. Those appointments are discussed in chapter 3.

51. See U.S. Department of Justice, *EOIR Announces 46 New Immigration Judges* (July 17, 2020), https://perma.cc/K3PP-BEJ9.

One of the other forty-six had worked at DHS but not at ICE. See also the description of the backgrounds of immigration judges appointed by Attorney General Sessions, discussed in chapter 3.

52. Department of Justice, *Appellate Procedures and Decisional Finality in Immigration Proceedings*, 85 Fed. Reg. 52491, at 52512 (Aug. 26, 2020). As Judge Ashley Tabaddor, President of the National Association of Immigration Judges said, "Imagine going to a court where you've been charged by a prosecutor and when you come to court you find that . . . the prosecutor can come in and overrule the judge." Stephen Franklin, *The Revolt of the Judges, American Prospect* (June 23, 2020). The validity of the regulation was challenged in a lawsuit filed just before it was scheduled to become effective. *Catholic Legal Immigration Network v. Executive Office for Immigration Review,* Case 21-94 (D. D.C. 2021).

53. Department of Justice, *Procedures for Asylum and Withholding of Removal*, 85 Fed. Reg. 59692 (Sept. 23, 2020).

54. The USCIS requirement is discussed in chapter 3.

55. 85 *Fed. Reg.* 59694.

56. Id.

57. "You must submit reasonably available corroborative evidence showing (1) the general conditions in the country from which you are seeking asylum, and (2) the specific facts on which you are relying to support your claim. If evidence supporting your claim is not reasonably available or you are not providing such corroboration at this time, you must explain why, using Form I-589, Supplement B, or additional sheets of paper. Supporting evidence may include but is not limited to newspaper articles, affidavits of witnesses or experts, medical and/or psychological records, doctors' statements, periodicals, journals, books, photographs, official documents, or personal statements or live testimony from witnesses or experts." Department of Homeland Security, *Instructions for Completing Form I-589, Application for Asylum and Withholding of Removal,* https://perma.cc/CK59 -A8VX.

58. In the law school clinic where the authors have worked, successful applicants often file five hundred to seven hundred pages of supporting documents, such as medical proof of their torture, ar-

rest records from their home country, witness statements, expert declarations, and published reports about human rights conditions in the applicant's country.

59. See Aaron Reichlin-Melnick, "Proposed 15-Day Filing Rule for Asylum Seekers Is Designed to Be Impossible," *Immigration Impact*, Sept. 24, 2020, https://perma.cc/5DYD-UAAB; *Order for Preliminary Injunction, National Immigrant Justice Center v. Executive Office for Immigration Review*, Case 21-56 (D.C., 2021).

60. Department of Homeland Security and Department of Justice, *Procedures for Asylum and Bars to Asylum Eligibility*, 85 Fed. Reg. 67202 (Oct. 21, 2020).

61. *Pangea Legal Svcs. v. Dept. of Homeland Security*, 2020 WL 6802474 (N.D. Cal. 2020); and, in the same case, *Order Converting TRO to Preliminary Injunction*, Nov. 24, 2020, https://perma.cc/CWH8-C6KU.

62. 8 C.F.R. Sec. 1208.12, as proposed at 85 *Fed. Reg.* 59699.

63. Id.

64. Recall the efforts, described in chapter 3, of a senior DHS official to alter intelligence reports to make asylum less available.

65. *Matter of J-G-T-*, 28 I. & N. Dec. 97 (BIA, 2020).

66. *Matter of A-C-A-A-*, 28 I. & N. Dec. 84 (A.G., 2020).

67. Department of Justice, *Organization of the Executive Office for Immigration Review*, 84 Fed. Reg. 44537 (Aug. 26, 2020) (interim rule).

68. Department of Justice, *Organization of the Executive Office for Immigration Review*, 85 Fed. Reg. 69465 (Nov. 3, 2020) (final rule).

69. *Organization of the Executive Office for Immigration Review*, at 69466.

70. *Organization of the Executive Office for Immigration Review*, at 69467, and n. 3.

71. Departments of Homeland Security and Justice, *Procedures for Asylum and Withholding of Removal*, 85 Fed. Reg. 80274 (Dec, 11, 2020).

72. *Ghahremani v. Gonzales*, 498 F. 3d 993, 999 (9th Cir. 2007).

73. 8 C.F.R. Sec. 1003.23(b) and (f), as they would be amended by the proposed regulation, Department of Justice, *Motions to Reopen and Reconsider*, 85 Fed. Reg. 75942 (Nov. 27, 2020) (Notice of Proposed Rulemaking).

74. See Ingrid Eagly and Steven Shafer, *A National Study of Access to Counsel in Immigration Court*, 165 *Univ. of Pennsylvania L. Rev.* 1 (2015).

75. Department of Justice, *Good Cause for a Continuance in Immigration Proceedings*, 85 *Fed. Reg.* 75925 (Nov. 27, 2020). The deadline for public comments was December 28, in the week between Christmas and New Year, which most advocates' offices would be closed.

Chapter 6

1. Edward M. Kennedy, *Refugee Act of 1980*, 15 *Int'l Migration Rev.*, 141, 145 (1981).

2. Sen. Kennedy, *Cong. Rec.–Senate* 3757 (Feb. 26, 1980) (Conference report submitted in Senate and agreed to).

3. Our legislative recommendations address only the issues pertinent to the asylum system. The Biden administration might want to try to persuade Congress to enact a comprehensive immigration reform bill such as the one passed by the Senate in 2013, but that is beyond the scope of this book.

4. Biden-Harris, *The Biden Plan for Securing Our Values as a Nation of Immigrants*, https://joebiden.com/immigration/.

5. Refugee Protection Act of 2019, S. 2936, 116th Cong. (Nov. 19, 2019), H.R. 5219, 116th Cong. (Nov. 21, 2019); see also *Biden-Sanders Unity Task Force Recommendations*, at 38–41, 102–10 (2020), https://joebiden.com/wp-content/uploads/2020/07/UNITY-TASK-FORCE-RECOMMENDATIONS.pdf/.

6. We recommend four thoughtful and timely reports on broader changes to the immigration system: T. Alexander Aleinikoff and Donald Kerwin, *Improving the U.S. Immigration System in the First Year of the Biden Administration*, Zolberg Institute on Migration and Mobility, New School, and Center for Migration Studies of New York (Nov. 2020); American Bar Association, *Achieving America's Immigration Promise* (Jan. 2021); Doris Meissner, *Rethinking the U.S.-Mexico Border Immigration Enforcement System: A Policy Road Map*, Migration Policy Institute (Oct. 2020); and Sarah Pierce and Jessica Bolter, *Dismantling and Reconstructing the U.S. Immigration System: A Catalog of Changes Under the*

Trump Presidency, Migration Policy Institute (July 2020), www
.migrationpolicy.org/research/us-immigration-system-chang-
es-trump-presidency. We also recommend *Asylum Under Attack*,
a law review article that describes changes to the asylum system under the Trump administration and makes proposals for
reform. Lindsay Harris, *Asylum Under Attack, 67 Loyola L. Rev.*
(2020).

7. It is possible that all regulations issued and actions taken by the
Department of Homeland Security after April 10, 2019, were
invalid. The DHS inspector general is currently determining
whether actions taken after Kirstjen Nielsen's resignation were
invalid because her successors, including Chad Wolf and Kenneth Cuccinelli, were not properly designated to serve upon her
resignation. U.S. Government Accountability Office, *Decision,
Matter of: Department of Homeland Security—Legality of Service of
Acting Secretary of Homeland Security and Service of Senior Official
Performing the Duties of Deputy Secretary of Homeland Security,
File B-331650* (Aug. 14, 2020), https://perma.cc/6BFA-YJ7G.
Several federal district courts have held that Chad Wolf was improperly appointed under the Federal Vacancies Reform Act of
1998, 5 U.S.C. § 3345 at seq. (FVRA), so he did not have authority to issue the memo that terminated Deferred Action for
Childhood Arrivals. The decisions are collected in the opinion
granting a preliminary injunction in *Pangea Legal Services v. Department of Homeland Security,* Case No. 20-9253 (N.D.Ca. Jan.
8, 2021). Another federal district court has held that three policies announced by Kenneth Cuccinelli relating to scheduling
credible fear interviews were invalid because he was improperly
appointed under the FVRA. *L-M-M- v. Cuccinelli,* No. 19-2676
(D.D.C., Mar. 1, 2020).

8. 142 *Cong. Rec.* S11491 (daily ed., Sept. 27, 1996). Senator Orrin Hatch stated, "I believe [the expedited removal process] will
provide adequate protections to legitimate asylum claimants
who arrive in the United States. If it does not, let me say that I
will remain committed to revisiting this issue to ensure that
we continue to provide adequate protection to those fleeing
persecution."

9. 142 *Cong. Rec.* S11491 (daily ed., Sept. 27, 1996).

10. See chapter 4.

11. Refugee Protection Act of 2019, at § 134, 136. Again, a new administration can and should make these changes immediately upon taking office.

12. See chapter 4.

13. Biden-Harris, *Biden Plan*.

14. See chapter 4.

15. Joseph Biden, tweet, @JoeBiden (Jan. 25, 2020); Dara Lind, *Trump Got What He Wanted at the Border, Would Biden Undo It?* Pro Publica (Oct. 28, 2020), https://perma.cc/G2JW-MPQK. For a thoughtful proposal on how to end the MPP, see HIAS, *Roadmap to Recovery: A Path Forward After the Remain in Mexico Program* (Jan. 2021), https://www.hias.org/sites/default/files/hias_mpp_report_exec_summary.pdf.

16. As noted in chapter 4, more than 65,000 asylum seekers have been forced into MPP since the program started. We have not been able to find reliable statistics counting the number of people who remain in vulnerable situations on the Mexican side of the southern border. The most recent count of individuals in the MPP program, in December 2020, was 22,777. Stephanie Leutert and Savitri Arvey, *Migrant Protection Protocols Update: December 2020* (Strauss Center for International Security and Law, Univ. of Texas), https://www.strausscenter.org/wp-content/uploads/MPPUpdate_December2020.pdf Of that number, we do not know how many asylum seekers remain at the border, because some have abandoned their claims, but likely far fewer than 23,000 remain. *Id.*

17. Biden-Harris, *Biden Plan*. See also chapter 4.

18. Senator Leahy and Representative Lofgren's bills provide a presumption of liberty for asylum seekers, pending their immigration court hearings, unless they are flight risks or threats to another person or the community. Refugee Protection Act, at § 133(a)(2)(B).

19. Refugee Protection Act, at § 133. Their bills provide that the decision to detain cannot be based solely on pending criminal charges, a lack of identity evidence, or a lack of preexisting

community ties with the United States. They also require that detained asylum seekers must have access to custody redetermination hearings every sixty days or on a showing of changed circumstances or good cause.

20. A new administration should quickly terminate the Trump administration's family separation practices, which have continued even since Trump's executive order purportedly ended them. Young Center, *Family Separation Is Not Over* (June 25, 2020), www.theyoungcenter.org/report-family-separation-is-not-over. Any separated children should be immediately reunited with their parents. Vice President Biden's plan would end prosecution of parents and prioritize reunification of children still separated from their families. Biden-Harris, *Biden Plan.* The Leahy and Lofgren bills forbid the prosecution for unlawful entry of any person who has applied for asylum or indicates an intent to apply for asylum while their claim is pending, and until their claim is denied or they fail to meet a time limit for filing. Refugee Protection Act, at § 137.

21. See chapter 4.

22. Art. 31(1) of the Refugee Convention reads, "The Contracting States shall not impose penalties, on account of their illegal entry or presence, on refugees who, coming directly from a territory where their life or freedom was threatened in the sense of Article 1, enter or are present in their territory without authorization, provided they present themselves without delay to the authorities and show good cause for their illegal entry or presence."

23. *Joe Biden Agenda for the Latino Community,* ("Biden will end [Trump's detrimental asylum policies], starting with Trump's Migrant Protection Protocols and Safe Third Country Agreements."), https://perma.cc/DM7H-RASU; Camilo Montoya-Galvez, *Biden plans sweeping reversal of Trump's immigration agenda, from deportations to asylum policy,* CBS News (Nov. 11, 2020) ("A source familiar with the Biden team's planning said the incoming administration will withdraw from the three bilateral agreements Mr. Trump brokered with Guatemala, El Salvador and Honduras that allow the U.S. to send rejected asylum-seekers to those countries and have them seek refuge there."), https://

perma.cc/ZL28-645T. See also also chapter 4.

24. See the agreement with Guatemala "on cooperation regarding the examination of protection claims," Art. 8, Clause 2 (providing for termination of the agreement on three months' notice), https://perma.cc/5CJC-DXDW.

25. See chapter 4.

26. *Letter to HHS Secretary Azar and CDC Director Redfield Signed by Leaders of Public Health Schools, Medical Schools, Hospitals, and Other U.S. Institutions* (May 18, 2020), https://www.public health.columbia.edu/public-health-now/news/public-health -experts-urge-us-officials-withdraw-order-enabling-mass-expul sion-asylum-seekers.

27. See chapters 3 and 5.

28. Jaya Ramji-Nogales, Andrew I. Schoenholtz, and Philip G. Schrag, *Refugee Roulette*, 60 *Stan. L. Rev.* 295, 383–84 (2007); Andrew I. Schoenholtz, Philip G. Schrag, and Jaya Ramji-Nogales, *Lives in the Balance*, 216–19 (New York: New York University Press, 2004). See, e.g., *Statement of Judge A. Ashley Tabaddor, President, National Association of Immigration Judges, Before the Senate Judiciary Committee, Border Security and Immigration Subcommittee*, at 11 (Apr. 18, 2018), www.judiciary.senate.gov /imo/media/doc/04-18-18%20Tabaddor%20Testimony.pdf. Former vice president Biden's immigration plan would double the number of immigration judges, court staff, and interpreters. Biden-Harris, *Biden Plan*.

29. Schoenholtz et al., *Lives*, 117, 122–23.

30. U.S. Government Accountability Office, *Agencies Have Taken Actions to Help Ensure Quality in the Asylum Adjudication Process, but Challenges Remain*, GAO-08-935 (Sept. 25, 2008); Chris Guthrie, Jeffrey J. Rachlinski, and Andrew J. Wistrich, *Blinking on the Bench: How Judges Decide Cases*, 93 *Cornell L. Rev.* 1, 35 (2007).

31. U.S. Citizenship and Immigration Services (USCIS) faced a backlog of over 300,000 asylum cases at the end of fiscal year 2019. USCIS, *Annual Report on the Impact of the Homeland Security Act on Immigration Functions Transferred to the Department of Homeland Security*, at 12 (Apr. 29, 2020), www.uscis.gov/sites /default/files/reports-studies/Annual-Report-on-the-Impact

-of-the-Homeland-Security-Act-on-Immigration-Functions
-Transferred-to-the-DHS-FY19-Signed-Dated-4.29.20.pdf.
See also USCIS, Asylum Division, *Quarterly Meeting Agenda,
May 20, 2019*, at 2 (explaining that the Asylum Division has re-
ceived more cases and referrals than it has staff to complete for
the past five years), www.uscis.gov/sites/default/files/USCIS
/Outreach/Notes%20from%20Previous%20Engagements
/PED_AsylumStakeholderMeetingQA_05202019.pdf. The
immigration courts had in the range of 1 million cases of all types
in the backlog at the end of fiscal year 2019. U.S. Department
of Justice (DOJ), Office of the Inspector General, *Audit of the
Executive Office for Immigration Review's Fiscal Year 2019 Financial
Management Practices*, at 9 (June 2020), https://oig.justice.gov
/sites/default/files/reports/a20068.pdf.

32. Ramji-Nogales et al., *Refugee Roulette*, 295, 383.

33. Given that the immigration court faced a backlog of nearly 1.3
million immigration cases—the largest backlog in its—in fiscal
year 2021, the hiring of more immigration judges is an urgent
priority. *Transactional Records Access Clearinghouse, FY 2021 Begins with Largest Immigration Court Backlog on Record* (Nov. 24,
2020), https://trac.syr.edu/whatsnew/email.201124.html

34. Biden-Harris, *Biden Plan*. We expect from prior conversations
with immigration judges and asylum officers that the adjudicators would welcome such training. Ramji-Nogales et al., *Refugee
Roulette*, 295, 381; Schoenholtz et al., *Lives*, at 117, 218–19.

35. Schoenholtz et al., *Lives*, 86–87, 215–16.

36. See chapter 3.

37. The Associate Director of USCIS is required to maintain a human rights documentation center under 8 C.F.R. Sec. 208.1(b).
The former Resource Information Center, now known as the Research Unit, is currently designated to perform this function. US-
CIS, *Researching and Using Country of Origin Information in RAIO
Adjudications: Training Module*, 19–20, https://www.uscis.gov
/sites/default/files/document/foia/COI_LP_RAIO.pdf. See
also EOIR, Country Conditions Research page, https://www
.justice.gov/eoir/country-conditions-research.

38. Biden-Harris, *Biden Plan*.

39. See chapter 3.
40. American Bar Association, Commission on Immigration, *2019 Update Report*, at (2) 12, 17, 20, (6) 1, 16 (Mar. 2019).
41. Biden-Harris, *Biden Plan*.
42. See the discussion in chapter 3, *Matter of Acosta*, 19 I. & N. Dec. 211, 234 (BIA, 1985), and *Gatimi v. Holder*, 578 F.3d 611 (7th Cir., 2009). In *Gatimi*, the court determined that a BIA requirement that a group had to have "social visibility," was not authorized by the Refugee Act. The BIA later renamed "social visibility" as "social distinction" to reflect the fact that groups such as girls threatened with genital cutting did not need to have "ocular" visibility. *Matter of M-E-V-G-*, 26 I. & N. Dec. 227 (BIA, 2014). But the terminological change does not affect the court's analysis.
43. See the discussion in chapter 3, *Matter of Acosta*, 19 I. & N. Dec. 211, 234 (BIA, 1985).
44. See chapter 4.
45. See chapter 4.
46. See chapter 3.
47. See chapter 5.
48. These were discussed in chapters 3, 4, and 5.
49. *Encino Motorcars LLC v. Navarro*, 136 S. Ct. 2117, 2125–26 (2016); *FCC v. Fox Television Stations, Inc.*, 556 U.S. 502, 515 (2009).
50. *Dept. of Homeland Security v. Regents of the Univ. of California*, 591 U.S. 140 S. Ct. 1891 (2020). This was the recent Deferred Action for Childhood Arrivals case (invalidating the Trump administration's rescission of immigration benefits for the innocent children of certain undocumented migrants). In dissent, Justice Clarence Thomas observed that under the Court's ruling, "Even if the agency lacked authority to effectuate the changes [in its original regulation], the changes cannot be undone by the same agency in a successor administration unless the successor provides sufficient policy justifications to the satisfaction of this Court." This decision was built on enduring case law establishing that a regulation that rescinds or changes an earlier regulation is, nevertheless, a new regulation that is subject to the same procedures

of the APA, including the need for "reasoned decision-making," and then subject to judicial review. See *Encino Motorcars LLC v. Navarro*, 136 S. Ct. 2117, 2125–26 (2016); *FCC v. Fox Television Stations, Inc.*, 556 U.S. 502, 515 (2009); and *Motor Vehicles Mfr.s Ass'n of United States v. State Farm Mut. Auto. Ins. Co.*, 463 U.S. 29 (1983).

51. E.g., in the case involving Deferred Action for Childhood Arrivals, thousands of "dreamers" had relied on the program that President Obama had created to provide benefits for them. The Trump administration could not cancel the program without giving valid reasons for doing so. In the earlier 2016 *Encino Motors* case, the Obama administration decided, contrary to prior policy in effect since 1978, that automobile dealers' "service advisors" (who sell maintenance and repair services to customers) were not exempt from overtime pay requirements in the Fair Labor Standards Act. *Encino Motorcars LLC v. Navarro*, 136 S. Ct. 2117, 2125-26 (2016). The Supreme Court rejected the change, stating that "a reasoned explanation is needed for disregarding facts and circumstances that underlay or were engendered by the prior policy." The Court reached that decision because dealers had relied for decades on the prior policy and had structured their compensation plans on the assumption that it would continue. In the *Fox Television* case, the Supreme Court also cited reliance in its explanation of when an agency must provide detailed justifications for a policy change. *FCC v. Fox Television Stations, Inc.*, 556 U.S. 502, 515 (2009): "The agency need not always provide a more detailed justification than what would suffice for a new policy created on a blank slate. Sometimes it must—when, for example, its new policy rests upon factual findings that contradict those which underlay its prior policy; or when its prior policy has engendered serious reliance interests that must be taken into account."

52. In practice, for each modification or outright rejection of an old regulation, some individual or small group of policy makers would have to write the new rule, a justification and explanation, and statements to show that the rule complied with many statutory requirements such as those in the Paperwork Reduction

Act, the Regulatory Flexibility Act, and the Unfunded Mandates Reform Act of 1995. The rule itself might be brief, but lengthy justifications, including empirical and statistical data, could help the rule to survive judicial review. Some of the Trump administration's justifications for its immigration rules exceeded 100 typed pages in length. The Biden administration's task of modifying or repealing the regulations will be facilitated, however, by the fact that many individuals and organizations provided well-reasoned critiques, with empirical backup, in response to the Trump regulations when they were proposed.

Then the rule would go through the interagency clearance process. Working groups consisting of representatives from many interested policy agencies would study the rule, and each might insist on changes. These working groups would consist of experts, lawyers, and other policy officials from the agencies that administer the policies, including USCIS, ICE, and CBP from DHS; EOIR and possibly the Office of Immigration Litigation from DOJ; and the Domestic Policy Council. The working group members from each agency would bring their own perspectives. Disagreements that could not be resolved at the working group level could be taken to meetings of assistant secretaries or their deputies, and continued disagreements could be taken to meetings of "principals" (cabinet members), and ultimately might have to be resolved by President Biden.

After many iterations over a period of months, a draft rule would go to the Office of Management and Budget, which might require further revision. Finally, the proposed rule would be published in the Federal Register for public notice and comment, as required by the APA. For the next thirty to sixty days, the originating agencies would receive comments from interested states, corporations, nonprofit organizations, and individual members of the public.

After the notice and comment period, the agencies would have to write and coordinate responses to every type of comment that they received, including every type of objection, a process that could consume many more months. They would need to adjust their proposed new policy if the comments revealed flaws in their thinking or justification. Then a final regulation could be published in the *Federal Register*.

53. After all that, the final rule might not take effect if objectors sue the agencies in federal court to overturn the regulation, arguing that the agencies had not sufficiently justified their reasons for changing federal policy, just as many states and organizations sued to invalidate regulations during the Trump administration. If they lost those cases at the trial level, they could appeal, possibly all the way up to the Supreme Court.

54. See chapter 5.

55. See chapter 4.

56. See chapter 4.

57. See chapter 3.

58. See chapter 5.

59. See chapter 3.

60. The proposed regulation gives asylum seekers thirty days to complete the blank spaces; if the applicant does not meet this deadline, it would deem an application abandoned. See chapter 5.

61. Negating this regulation is less urgent only because the government has been enjoined from enforcing it, and a stay of that injunction was denied by the Supreme Court. But if the courts were to reverse the injunction, that could change.

62. See chapters 4 and 5.

63. The pending suits include challenges to the new fees for asylum applications and employment authorization and the longer waiting period before an asylum applicant can work, the new standards for credible fear determinations, Trump's family separation policy, the abrogation of the Flores Settlement Agreement, the denial of bond to those who received positive credible fear determinations, the consignment of minors from ORR custody to ICE detention when a child becomes eighteen, the practice of metering, the denial of asylum to those who entered between border posts, the denial of asylum to those who did not apply in another country through which they passed, the MPP program, and the imposition of bars to asylum for convictions of minor crimes.

64. See Philip G. Schrag, *Baby Jails: The Fight to End the Incarceration*

of Refugee Children in America (Berkeley: University of California Press, 2020).

65. See *Pangea Legal Services v. Department of Homeland Security,* Case No. 20-9253 (N.D.Ca.).

66. *Las Americas Immigrant Advocacy Center v. Trump,* Case 3:19-cv-02051 (D. Or). In July, 2020, the court denied the government's motion to dismiss all but one of the plaintiffs' claims in the case. *Opinion and Order in Las Americas Immigrant Advocacy Center v. Trump,* Case 3:19-cv-02051 (D. Or., 2020), https://perma.cc/QGS5-BCZA.

67. The only claim in the *Las Americas* case that the court dismissed (on jurisdictional grounds) was the claim that the Department of Justice had created certain asylum-free zones, cities in which asylum was almost never granted. But that issue could be revived on appeal, so it too could be settled by a Biden administration.

68. S, 2936 (116th Cong., 1st Sess.) (Nov. 21, 2019); H.R. 5210 (116th Cong., 1st Sess.) (Nov. 21, 2019).

69. Some of our recommendations are also suggested by a recent report published by the Center for Migration Studies and the Zolberg Institute on Migration and Mobility. Center for Migration Studies and Zolberg Institute on Migration and Mobility, *Improving the U.S. Immigration System in the First Year of the Biden Administration* (2020), https://perma.cc/65WQ-2ZN3. A recent report by the Migration Policy Institute also makes many useful suggestions for reforming immigration enforcement at the southern border, with particular emphasis on changes in asylum law and policy. Doris Meissner, *Rethinking the U.S.-Mexico Border Immigration Enforcement System: A Policy Road Map (2020),* https://www.migrationpolicy.org/research/rethinking-us-mexico-border-immigration-enforcement.

70. This provision should eliminate the "social distinction" and "particularity" requirements for the identification of social groups as well as overturning the decisions by attorneys general Sessions and Barr to limit asylum for domestic violence victims and those persecuted because of animus toward their relatives.

71. The Leahy and Lofgren bills would return to the *Acosta* standard of immutability and past experience but also include a provision

that members of a social group must be "perceived as a group by society." We do not agree with the latter provision. Refugee Protection Act, at § 101.

72. Recall that in the omnibus regulation discussed in chapter 5, the Trump administration attempted to prohibit immigration judges from granting asylum to victims of persecution imposed on the because of their gender. A statutory specification of gender as a protected ground would prevent a future administration from enacting such a rule. Gender is not a ground listed in the Refugee Convention, but U.S. law, though based on the convention, departs from it in several ways, including the creation of asylum as a durable rather than temporary measure of protection.

73. The Leahy and Lofgren bills include the following language, which we endorse: "Where past or feared persecution by a non-state actor is unrelated to a protected asylum ground, the causal nexus link is established if the state's failure to protect the asylum applicant from the nonstate actor is on account of a protected asylum ground." Refugee Protection Act, at § 101.

74. Zora Franicevic, Ian M. Kysel, and Thomas G. Shannan, *Salvaging U.S. Refugee Law in 2021: The Case for Tackling the Problem of Discretionary Asylum,* Just Security (Jan. 20, 2021), https://www.justsecurity.org/74263/salvaging-us-refugee-law-in-2021-the-case-for-tackling-the-problem-of-discretionary-asylum/.

75. This regulation would overturn any implication suggested by the attorney general's action in *Matter of E-F-H-L-* or in the Trump administration's effort to authorize immigration judges, by regulation, to order deportation of asylum seekers because their written statements alone did not seem to justify a grant of asylum. See chapters 3 and 5.

76. Refugee Protection Act, at § 103. See Andrew I. Schoenholtz, Philip G. Schrag, Jaya Ramji-Nogales, and James P. Dombach, *Rejecting Refugees: Homeland Security's Administration of the One-Year Bar to Asylum,* 52 *Wm. & Mary L. Rev.* 651 (2011–12).

77. The Trump administration's expulsion of asylum seekers under this statute is wholly inconsistent with later-in-time statutes such as the Refugee Act and the Trafficking Victims Protection Reauthorization Act of 2008.

78. The Trump administration claimed that the authority for MPPs derives from the Immigration and Nationality Act § 235(b)(2)(C): "Treatment of aliens arriving from contiguous territory. In the case of an alien described in subparagraph (A) who is arriving on land (whether or not at a designated port of arrival) from a foreign territory contiguous to the United States, the [secretary of homeland security] may return the alien to that territory pending a proceeding under section 1229a of this title." Even if the Biden administration does not withdraw the government's appeal and the Supreme Court agrees with the Trump administration's interpretation, the fact remains that, as explained in chapter 4, Congress did not intend this provision to apply to asylum seekers and should eliminate it.

79. As noted above, Congress should also heed President Biden's call to double the number of immigration judges to clear the backlog of more than a million cases. Biden-Harris, *Biden Plan*.

80. This proposal has been made in more detail by Doris Meissner, former Commissioner of the Immigration and Naturalization Service, and Sarah Pierce of the Migration Policy Institute. Doris Meissner and Sarah Pierce, *Policy Solutions to Address Crisis at Border Exist, But Require Will and Staying Power to Execute,* Migration Policy Institute (April 2019), https://www.migrationpolicy.org/news/policy-solutions-address-crisis-border-exist-require-will-staying-power. Although it might add some procedural complexity as cases are shifted back to the Asylum Office from the immigration courts, it should also relieve the caseload of the immigration courts.

81. Ingrid V. Eagly and Steven Shafer, *Measuring In Absentia Removal in Immigration Court,* 168 *Penn L. Rev.* 817 (2020); Nina Siulc and Noelle Smart, *Evidence Shows that Most Immigrants Appear for Immigration Court Hearings, Vera Inst. of Justice* (Oct. 2020), https://www.vera.org/downloads/publications/immigrant-court-appearance-fact-sheet.pdf; Emily Ryo, *Representing Immigrants: The Role of Lawyers in Immigration Bond Hearings,* 52 *Law & Society Review* 503 (2018); Ingrid V. Eagly and Steven Shafer, *A National Study of Access to Counsel in Immigration Court,* 164 Penn. L. Rev. 1 (2015); Ramji-Nogales et al., *Refugee Rou-*

lette, 295, 384; Schoenholtz et al., *Lives*, 117, 216–17; Andrew I. Schoenholtz and Jonathan Jacobs, *The State of Asylum Representation: Ideas for Change*, 16 Geo. Immig. L. J. 739–64 (2002).

82. Refugee Protection Act, at §113: "The Attorney General may appoint or provide counsel to aliens in any proceeding conducted under section 235(b), 236, 238, 240, or 241 or any other section of this Act." Vulnerable applicants include those with a disability, survivors of abuse, torture, and violence, and other circumstances. The bills require that the government facilitate access to counsel for detained applicants. The bills also require that immigrants receive a copy of their A file at the beginning of proceedings, a small step that would go a long way in ensuring confrontation rights in asylum hearings. See also American Bar Association, Commission on Immigration, *2019 Update Report: Reforming the Immigration System—Proposals to Promote Independence, Fairness, Efficiency, and Professionalism in the Adjudication of Removal Cases*, at (5) 25–28 (Mar. 2019).

83. *Funding Attorneys for Indigent Removal Proceedings Act*, S. 2389, 116th Cong., 1st Sess., introduced July 31, 2019, www.congress.gov/bill/116th-congress/senate-bill/2389/text.

84. The Leahy and Lofgren bills allocate funding to DOJ and DHS efforts to facilitate access to counsel for detainees and the continuation of the Legal Orientation Programs that provide asylum seekers with basic information on procedures and rights. They further require DOJ to submit an annual report on access to counsel in immigration proceedings to Congress. Refugee Protection Act, at § 113.

85. Steven Legomsky, *Fear and Loathing in Congress and the Courts: Immigration and Judicial Review*, 78 *Texas L. Rev.* 1615 (2000); American Bar Association, Commission on Immigration, *2019 Update Report*, at (4) 7 (Mar. 2019). The Leahy and Lofgren bills include a revision of 8 U.S.C. 1252(b) that enables federal courts of appeals to review final orders of removal under the abuse of discretion and substantial evidence standards. Refugee Protection Act, at § 132.

86. Refugee Protection Act, at § 132 (2).

INDEX

ABOUT THE AUTHORS

Andrew I. Schoenholtz is a professor from practice at Georgetown Law School, where he codirects the Center for Applied Legal Studies, the asylum clinic in which students represent refugees fleeing persecution who seek asylum in the United States. He also directs the school's Human Rights Institute and its Certificate in Refugees and Humanitarian Emergencies program. He has taught courses on refugee law and policy, refugees and humanitarian emergencies, and immigration law and policy, as well as a practicum on the rights of detained immigrants. Before teaching at Georgetown, he served as deputy director of the U.S. Commission on Immigration Reform. He also practiced immigration, asylum, and international law with the Washington law firm Covington & Burling. He has conducted fact-finding missions in Haiti, Cuba, Ecuador, Germany, Croatia, Bosnia, Malawi, and Zambia to study the root causes of forced migration, refugee protection, long-term solutions to mass migration emergencies, and humanitarian relief operations. He researches and writes regularly on refugee law and policy. His publications include *The Promise and Challenge of Humanitarian Protection in the United States: Making Temporary Protected Status Work as a Safe Haven*; *The New Refugees and the Old Treaty: Persecutors and Persecuted in the Twenty-First Century*; *Lives in the Balance: Asylum Adjudication by the Department of Homeland Security* (coauthor);

Rejecting Refugees: Homeland Security's Administration of the One-Year Bar to Asylum (coauthor); *Refugee Roulette: Disparities in Asylum Adjudication* (coauthor); *Refugee Protection in the United States Post-September 11th*; *The Uprooted: Improving Humanitarian Responses to Forced Migration* ("Improving Legal Frameworks" chapter); and *Aiding and Abetting Persecutors: The Seizure and Return of Haitian Refugees in Violation of the UN Refugee Convention and Protocol.*

Jaya Ramji-Nogales is an associate dean for academic affairs and the I. Herman Stern Research Professor at Temple University's Beasley School of Law, where she teaches refugee law and policy and supervises the Temple Law Asylum Project. With her current coauthors, Andrew Schoenholtz and Philip Schrag, she has also published *Refugee Roulette: Disparities in Asylum Adjudication and Proposals for Reform*, an empirical study of adjudication at all four levels of the U.S. asylum system, and *Lives in the Balance: Asylum Adjudication by the Department of Homeland Security*, a quantitative and qualitative study of asylum adjudication before the Department of Homeland Security's Asylum Offices. Her current research examines refugee law under the Trump administration, including a comparative examination, with coauthor Tally Kritzman-Amir, of nationality bans in Israel and the United States; another comparative essay, with coauthor Iris Goldner Lang, on migration policy responses to the COVID-19 pandemic in the European Union and the United States; and an evaluation of refugee rhetoric in the United States since the Refugee Act of 1980. Her publications also seek to generate conversations about the concept of global migration law, including a symposium in the *American Journal of International Law Unbound*. In this vein, her work has uncovered the role of international law in constructing migration emergencies and critiqued human rights law as insufficiently attentive to the interests of undocumented migrants. She has also written articles on the situation of forced migrants under international criminal law and international humanitarian law as well as on regional migration law in Southeast Asia.

Philip G. Schrag is the Delaney Family Professor of Public Interest Law at Georgetown University. He teaches professional responsibility as well as codirecting the asylum law clinic with Andrew Schoenholtz. Before joining the Georgetown faculty in 1981, he was assistant counsel to the NAACP Legal Defense Educational Fund, the consumer advocate of the City of New York, a professor at Columbia University Law School, and the deputy general counsel of the U.S. Arms Control and Disarmament Agency. He is the author or coauthor of sixteen previous books and dozens of articles on immigration, nuclear arms control, consumer protection, legal ethics, and other issues of public policy. His books include *Baby Jails: The Fight to End the Incarceration of Refugee Children in America* (2020); *Ethical Problems in the Practice of Law* (with Lisa Lerman and Robert Rubinson, 2020); and *Asylum Denied: A Refugee's Struggle for Safety in America* (with David Ngaruri Kenney, 2008). He has been honored with Georgetown University's Presidential Award for Distinguished Teacher/Scholars, Equal Justice Works' Outstanding Law Faculty Member Award for leadership in nurturing a spirit of public service in legal education and beyond, Lexis/Nexis's Daniel Levy Memorial Award for outstanding achievement in immigration law, and the Association of American Law Schools' William Pincus Award for service to clinical legal education and its Deborah L. Rhode Award for contributions to increasing pro bono and public service opportunities in law schools through scholarship, service, and leadership.